THE STORY OF AMERICAN FURNITURE

THE MACMILLAN COMPANY
NEW YORK · BOSTON · CHICAGO · DALLAS
ATLANTA · SAN FRANCISCO

MACMILLAN AND CO., LIMITED
LONDON · BOMBAY · CALCUTTA · MADRAS
MELBOURNE

THE MACMILLAN COMPANY
OF CANADA, LIMITED
TORONTO

Illustration 1.

(Museum of City of New York)

A DUNCAN PHYFE DRAWING ROOM

THE STORY OF AMERICAN FURNITURE

BY THOMAS HAMILTON ORMSBEE
AUTHOR OF "EARLY AMERICAN FURNITURE MAKERS," ETC.

WITH THIRTY-ONE LINE DRAWINGS BY

ROBERT CURRY

AND

ONE HUNDRED AND SEVENTEEN

ILLUSTRATIONS

THE MACMILLAN COMPANY
PUBLISHERS NEW YORK
1941

Set up and printed. Published August, 1934.
Reprinted, May, 1935; September, 1937;
March, 1941.

PRINTED IN THE UNITED STATES OF AMERICA
NORWOOD PRESS LINOTYPE, INC.
NORWOOD, MASS., U.S.A.

To

HELEN AND MARY

We shared, peacefully,
our family antiques

ACKNOWLEDGMENT

WRITING a book on antique furniture without the interest and coöperation of a wide group of sympathetic individuals would be difficult if not impossible. For their kind assistance the author particularly wishes to thank: Ralph Sargent Bailey, managing editor, *Home and Field;* Homer Eaton Keyes, editor, *Antiques;* Charles Nagel, Jr., Curator of Decorative Arts, Yale University; Anna E. Smith, Curator, Museum of Fine Arts, Bowdoin College; Charles Messer Stow, antique editor, New York *Sun;* as well as those who have loaned illustrative material. These include: Museum of Fine Arts, Boston; Bowdoin Museum of Fine Arts, Brunswick, Maine; Gallery of Fine Arts, Yale University, New Haven, Connecticut, where the Mabel Brady Garvan Collection is housed which has been drawn on so extensively; Metropolitan Museum of Art, New York City; Museum of the City of New York; American Philosophical Society, Philadelphia; Pennsylvania Museum, Philadelphia; Essex Institute, Salem, Massachusetts; C. Sanford Bull; Dr. George P. Coopernail; Henry Ford; Mrs. Homer Eaton Keyes; Mrs. Louis L. Nichols; Mrs. William H. P. Phyfe; William Stuart Walcott, Jr.; American Art Association-Anderson Galleries, Inc.; Ginsburg & Levy, Inc., and Israel Sack.

INTRODUCTION

The original impetus for this book was had years ago in a Vermont farmhouse. A boy from Brooklyn, New York, where gilded parlor furniture designed a long time after Louis XVI and golden oak abortions from the Michigan furniture factories were considered the height of the desired, was having a great experience. He was visiting relatives who actually lived on the old farm.

While the live stock and farm work greatly impressed him, he was a crude Philistine and thought the furniture in the house comic and out-of-fashion. With youthful bad manners he made fun of the four-post beds, the Windsor chairs, Sheraton chests of drawers and Hepplewhite tables made of cherry and fancy grained maple. Then things happened! His hostess was a mild-mannered old lady, but not without fire. Would she let a young sprout from the city laugh at her furniture, most of which she had inherited? Not Aunt Lottie. If he did not know, it was time he learned; and she straightway set about making this boy understand what her furniture was, and what it stood for.

No doubt the old lady's feelings were hurt, and in recognizing her as my first mentor in the field of the antique I trust I am making tardy amends. Under her guidance I saw for the first time something of the charm of old furniture and dimly realized it was part of my heritage. What I would give today if Aunt Lottie's furniture were mine, is beside the point. In opening my eyes to what it meant and how it was made, she did me a better service.

Further, many others must have had like conversions to the antique years before mine. Whether we realize it or not, collecting old furniture has been going on in America for well over half a century. The first public display of antiques was a feature of the Centennial Exposition held in Philadelphia in 1876. The New England Cottage was where the first antique show of record was held.

Since then interest in and urge to possess what we now call Early American furniture has grown steadily year by year. At first it was a fad followed only by a few. Then more and more people who had old pieces stored away in attics and sheds, servants' rooms and cellars, acted in accord with Fingey Conner's motto ("Them as has 'em, wears 'em"), brought the old furniture out of retirement, and gave it a place of honor. Thus they were unconsciously building background for themselves and their children. Others with no attics to call on but with some spare money began to buy, here, there and everywhere. Some of the purchases were happy, and some later on were recognized as the dangerous mistakes of a little knowledge.

Somewhere along the line, collectors, near-collectors, and those with just a very few pieces realized that the old furniture had staying power that far surpassed the new factory product. Getting one's money's worth is a very common desire, and when, as a people, Americans began to recognize the fact that the old beds and bureaus, chairs and tables, desks and what will you, repaired by competent cabinetmakers, would outwear new pieces and did not cost much more, antique furniture collecting became the interest of the many.

At the same time many of the museums changed their manner of displaying their fine pieces and began to show them by periods in rooms taken from noteworthy old houses. Thus we learned the effects that could be accomplished by the use of antiques and saw these pieces in relation to houses and living. The American Wing of the Metropolitan Museum in New York was the first attempt of this kind, and its merit was so great that other museums straightway went and did likewise. Beyond the best possible display of their treasures these museums demonstrated that people with some antiques could use them to furnish their homes and have a personal museum which would be different than any other and at the same time be a practical, comfortable abode.

All of this is a statement of how the author happened to start collecting and studying antique furniture as well as something of the genesis of the vogue for the Early American generally. The purpose of this book will be to tell what to collect, where to find it, how to judge the merits of individual pieces and something of the development of the major items of our American furniture and the effects that the various style-trends had on them. By so doing he hopes that the result will be something of a handbook for those who want some antiques about the house. Veteran collectors and museum curators are not the audience addressed.

T. H. O.

Red Shingles,
Pound Ridge, N. Y.,
January 2, 1934.

CONTENTS

Part One

Part Two

ILLUSTRATIONS

LINE DRAWINGS IN TEXT

PART ONE

CHAPTER ONE

WHAT TO COLLECT, AND HOW TO DO IT

"I TRUST to my own eyes," Baron Duveen, the international art dealer, once testified in explaining the basis on which his firm, Duveen Brothers, reached decisions as to the merits of art objects. "I view each with an eye stored with the recollected vision of all the finest examples studied in over forty years," he added.

Whether one is going to gather just a few pieces of antique furniture or is more ambitious and has a houseful as the goal, Baron Duveen's statement is worth serious consideration. If one starts to buy old furniture without some standards of comparison, the early purchases are liable to be far from happy. On the other hand with the books that have been written; the issues of the magazine *Antiques* so ably edited by Homer Eaton Keyes since its establishment in 1922; weekly antiques departments in newspapers such as the New York *Sun* and the Boston *Transcript;* museums; exhibitions preceding auctions and the stocks of dealers big and little—with all these, any would-be collector can make a start at acquiring "an eye stored with recollected vision" that will pay dividends time and again. There is nothing like knowing what you see and knowing that you know it.

So can you spot the good pieces among the mediocre at a country auction, in a junk shop, or at a rummage sale. Similarly it will keep you from being deceived when a poor piece is displayed with much window dressing designed to enhance its merits.

A Terry clock out of an ash can and an Empire lyre-backed chair so loose in the joints that it was considered worthless and put out for the early morning call of the rubbish man are two extreme examples of furniture that have been mine for nothing because I recognized them despite surroundings. Part of the joy of collecting is the unknown chance that enters into it. Tomorrow, as I drive to the A. & P. store for coffee and chops, I may happen on a piece of the type to which I am partial—late 18th Century and early 19th Century farmhouse furniture; and if this should be my good luck I shall stop and at least investigate.

Several years ago, in a house just off Park Avenue in New York, I saw and recognized a sofa done in the best Duncan Phyfe manner. It was an ancestral piece, and my host had never thought of it as other than something from his grandfather's house on Maiden Lane. There was a certain warming satisfaction in being the first to recognize this piece that did not diminish when I later heard that a museum expert agreed with me.

So, if you purpose buying antique furniture, read and look first! If you are lucky enough to have a few heirlooms, use them for your laboratory specimens and identify them. Are they Puritan Century, William and Mary, Queen Anne, Chippendale, Hepplewhite, Sheraton, or Empire in line and construction? What is the wood or woods? Don't be thrown into confusion because the piece is a combination of several. The old cabinetmakers were inclined to use what they had, and, if mahogany or select native hardwood was running low, sometimes used other woods for the sides and underbody.

By this you will have begun your education in the antique and become enrolled for a course of study that can be followed as far as you like. Don't think that all there is to know about American furniture has been learned. Far from it! New and cogent data are developed all the time. You may stumble on and be able to identify a hitherto unknown cabinetmaker whose artistic skill and craftsmanship merit the rescue of his name and furniture from oblivion. If so, the chase through old newspapers, court records, and local history will be fascinating occupation for your spare time, and in the end you will have the satisfaction of having added something to the ever growing subject of Americana. For example, Chillicothe, Ohio, has a number of fine old houses of the Classic Revival. From what cabinetmaker's shop came their American Empire furnishings? An assignment for somebody! It might develop some very interesting angles.

But back to your eye and what you are going to collect. In the field of American furniture, collecting is not unlike ordering a luncheon. Individual taste is the all-governing factor. The farmhouse furniture of the 18th Century may have its appeal, especially if you are fortunate enough to live in a house of this type and period. Again, the pieces of the 17th Century made in New England, the Middle or Southern Colonies may possess special charm. Similarly the more sophisticated city-made furniture of the Chippendale, Hepplewhite, or Sheraton years or that of the American Empire, which was a further development of the third, may especially fit your abode. Or again you can be catholic and gather examples of all. It can be done, for our Early American pieces are good mixers, and pleasing effects can be had by judicious arrangement of examples varying as much as a hundred years in age.

But mere age is no criterion for passing on furniture. Its beauty depends primarily on line and proportion. A well-trained eye will save you from falling under the sway of pieces that are degenerate examples of what was once good or others that some one has endeavored to shift from one style period to another by rebuilding, added carving, or some other stupid and misguided effort. Each piece has within it internal evidences that tell one who can recognize them all about genuineness. These, plus the signs of normal wear, I have found so useful in my own collecting that the next chapter will be devoted to what I call antique detecting. Meanwhile, remember that line, proportion, and internal evidence of genuineness are the three cardinal things that govern judgment as to the merit of any piece.

The geographic location of the individual has great influence on what is collected. Of course, where money and time do not have to be considered, one can collect any type of furniture. If it does not flourish in the vicinity, the seeker can go where it does, or buy from dealers who bring it to him. But, for most of us, the practical course is to bend our attention to those things that can be picked up where we live.

A friend in Salt Lake City has found that many of the early Mormons brought with them pieces that still survive in the farmhouses within motoring distance. Accordingly she has gathered a most interesting collection of furniture that traveled West in covered wagons. Another, living in neighborly communion with the remnant of a Shaker settlement, has gradually furnished a house from top to bottom with examples of the severely plain chairs, tables, beds, and other pieces that the Shakers formerly made.

In each case the things collected fit their surroundings, and specializing in what is procurable locally brings results far ahead of what might come from gathering furniture generally found in other sections of the country. On the other hand neither of these people has proceeded without discrimination. Both have seen much that was poorly made, ungainly of shape, which they have left for others. Take so simple a thing as a drop-leaf table with tapered legs. If the legs are slender, and the reduction in size proceeds nicely from the bed to the floor, and the top is in proportion, it is good. Conversely, if the legs at the top are almost stout enough to support a piano, the table will be heavy and gross, no matter what the angle of the taper may be, except for a large banquet board. The finest mahogany or beautifully grained maple or birch cannot help such a piece. It lacks grace, and that is fatal.

Among my own things are two card tables of the type with a double top that folds back and rests on an out-swung leg. One is, I suppose, a farm version of the Chippendale. It is a New Hampshire piece made of yellow birch, but, to be candid, its legs are wrong. They are not square and the same size from top to bottom with a slight chamfer on the inner edge that

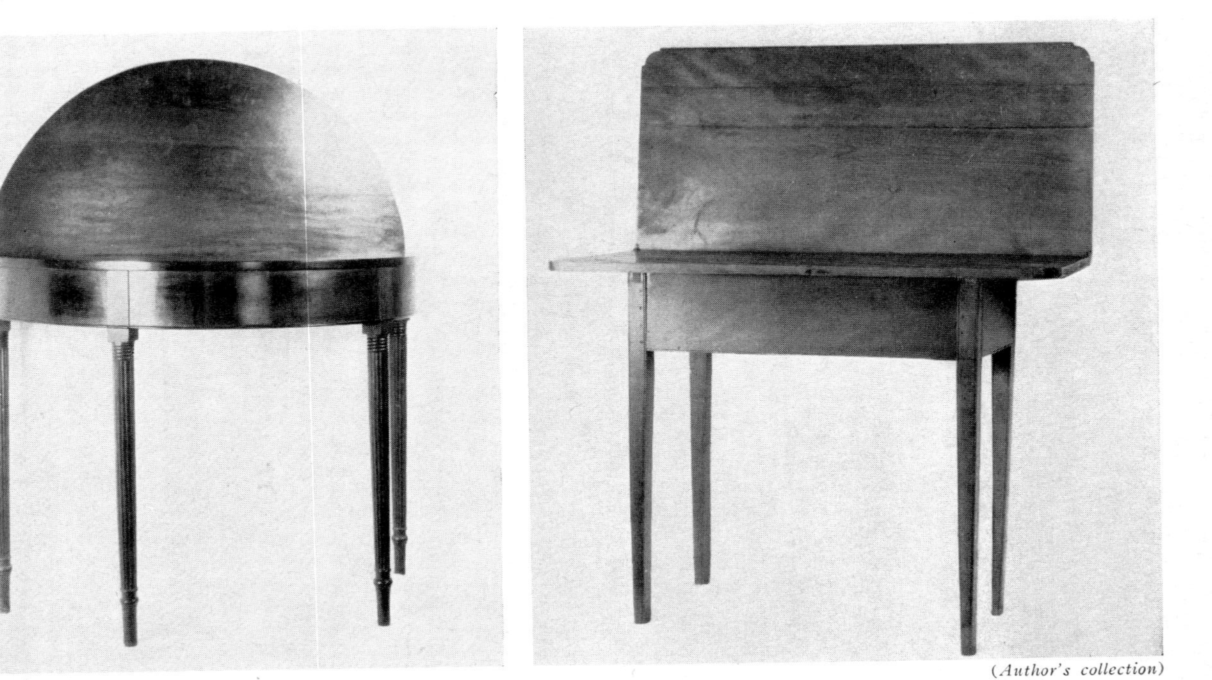

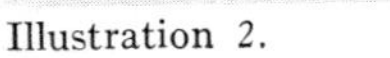

Illustration 2.

A B

(*Author's collection*)

FINE LINES PROCLAIM THE GOOD ANTIQUE

A, Sheraton card table of proper lines and proportions made in the first quarter of the 19th Century. B, Rural-made Chippendale card table about 1770–1780. The legs mar this piece noticeably. They should be square, not tapered.

would be truly Chippendale. They are not square with a slight downward taper that would be Hepplewhite in treatment. Instead they are oblong in cross section and taper so much as to be a little ungainly. The other table, probably fifty years younger, is of plain grained cherry, but each detail is in accord with the rest. The sweep of the half-round bed is bold but not too much so. The apron is in proportion to the size of the top, and the reeded round legs that diminish in size as they near the floor have a delicacy typical of the Sheraton design of which this piece is an example. Both are genuine pieces, but the former, even if it is mine, is not up to par for its type and style (*Illustration 2*).

In 1928 there was a remarkable auction in New York. One piece, known as the Van Pelt highboy, brought the record price for a single piece of furniture of $44,000. Somebody with a lot of money wanted it and somebody else with as much was on hand to fight for it. The real reason for this bidding battle royal was that this particular highboy was the finest example of the Philadelphia school of Chippendale disciples (*Illustration 3*). Its proportions were well balanced, the carving beautifully executed, and there was a gorgeous sweep to the bonnet top. The brasses were all original, as were the finials. The ball and claw cabriole legs were nicely sprung. In short, this gem of the Howard Reifsnyder collection might be defined as the sum of all the fine points existing in proper relation in a single piece. It represents excellence in American furniture of the highest degree. Hence the price, although other highboys made of just as good mahogany in equally good preservation could even then be bought for about a hundredth of the price because they lacked some if not all of its merits. They were, despite the fact that you or I would be glad to own them, just highboys, not the finest example of their type and style.

Excellence of design and execution is of course relative. The degree is naturally limited by the type and style of the particular piece. Why buy that which does not have as much

Illustration 3. *(American Art Assn.-Anderson Galleries)*

THE VAN PELT HIGHBOY

This was formerly in the Howard Reifsnyder collection. It is a typical Philadelphia piece dating *ca.* 1760–1770.

of this merit as possible? Why acquire pieces marred by bad design, clumsy execution, unwise mixture of two styles, or the debased and gross that characterize the decadent of any style or period? Duncan Phyfe was the prince of American cabinet-makers. His pieces done in the Sheraton and so-called Federal styles are things of entrancing beauty. Any collector that owns even one is indeed fortunate. Yet, in his later years, examples came from his shops so heavy and lacking in grace that the fact they are Phyfe is small consolation. Bad furniture is bad, whoever made it. He who buys such pieces acquires cats and dogs that will depreciate in ratio to the spread of knowledge of what is good design and proportion.

On the other hand there are pieces made of certain woods which are not yet as highly regarded as they should be. We have had our craze for pine. Curly and bird's-eye maple are much sought after, but for some unknown reason pieces made of yellow birch and cherry seem to have something of the bar sinister about them. Yet both woods are pleasing of grain and color. They just have not caught the popular fancy; but they will, and then the collector who has furniture of these woods can either keep it and gloat or send it to the auction block and take a handsome profit, provided the pieces have been gathered with wisdom and taste and have merit of line and proportion.

A nose for news is that quality which differentiates a good reporter from one who is simply a routine sort of being who happens to be working at journalism. The same holds for a born collector. He somehow realizes where he will find antiques and goes and does it. Some with this talent turn professional and, as antique dealers, make a living out of gathering old furniture. Others remain amateurs and utilize their gift only when they have money to spend on their hobby. But as a sense of line and proportion can be acquired, a person without the flair for finding good things can learn where to look.

Dealers' shops, particularly those of standing, are the logical first ports of call. With their reputation for the quality of the pieces handled, the prices must naturally be fairly high. They cannot afford to have sub-standard merchandise, and one must pay a premium for the knowledge that is behind their selections. For one who is willing to foot the bill such shops have much to offer. Here will be found practically all of the finest things—ultimate pieces, Joseph Hergesheimer is credited with calling them. Within the antique trade is a grapevine method of communication every bit as active as that existing in any prison and over it flashes news of outstanding finds that is radio-like in its speed. Because of it, such pieces do not remain long in other hands.

Then there are the lesser shops. Some of them are run by men graduated into the antique trade from the cabinet bench, who frequently have a sound practical knowledge of their wares. Others have gone into it from collecting or have just decided that running an antique shop is a good business. In the shops of the latter one who knows his antiques can sometimes pick up good things, unrecognized and underpriced.

Still further along are the men who have small shops but primarily devote themselves to supplying the needs of city dealers. If you happen on such a place before the urban antique shop proprietors have bought the good things unearthed by such a picker on his latest expedition, you will probably find some very desirable pieces and low prices; but such a dealer sells on a "buyer beware" basis. The collector must stand or fall by his own judgment. Further, he must know where to find these pickers. No dealer will tell him, and most collectors keep very quiet about the location of those they have discovered. Such a place, like the temple of stocks and bonds down Wall Street from Trinity Church, is no place for a lamb.

Further down the scale in antique channels of trade, there are two more types of stores where good pieces may occasionally be found. One is the standard secondhand store which carries a wide range of things, mostly junk. Then there are the rummage stores maintained by social agencies where the charitably inclined send their cast-off possessions. Finds of average good quality can be had at either. I once found a good Empire secretary in a secondhand store while a Good Will shop yielded a sofa of the same period. But these days such fortunate happenings are rare, because both are combed systematically by the pickers and small dealers who scout for themselves.

The auction sales are the other organized source of antiques and vary widely. Some, like the American Art Association-Anderson Galleries in New York, are marvelously managed institutions that issue impressive catalogues and hold exhibitions in advance of each sale that are well worth visiting. In such a way are outstanding collections put on the block and sold to the highest bidders.

Among the lesser auctioneers, some have their own rooms and sell a motley assemblage of things, good, bad, and indifferent. Others are more like the country auctioneers and go where the goods to be sold are. In either type of sale, good pieces of furniture may crop up, but the collector will usually be forced to compete sharply with pickers and dealers. These have an established practice, if an unknown "private party" bids, of forcing the price skyward to discourage his coming to another sale. They consider these sales their own preserve, which they are ready to defend with an occasional duel of this sort.

Away from the cities there are the auctioneers who go about holding sales at farms and the like. Such auctions were once the happy hunting ground of the collector with a little free time and money, but time has corrupted them. These country auctioneers now send their handbills to dealers in the vicinity, pickers, and city dealers. What is more, they are not above "salting" the sale with pieces that would not sell from unfortunate dealers' stocks. So country auctions are no longer so much of a collector's paradise. Besides, the number of collectors who follow these sales has greatly increased, with the result that today high prices and stiff competition as well as some furniture that is not what it seems are likely to be met.

Beyond antique shops and city or country auctions there is hunting your old furniture where it grows, which is almost as nice an art as finding a deer during the hunting season. You may or you may not succeed, but the logical places to look are the homes of families long established on the same site. There, whether in city, village, or on the farm, the furniture one really wants is most apt to be. But finding is one thing, and getting the owner to sell quite another. Here all the skill and tact of the experienced antiqueer come into play, and even then he may go away empty-handed.

"Nothing for sale, not if you covered it with dollar bills," said by lips that come to rest in a tight horizontal line, is a final answer. You might as well recognize it first as last. The only way around such an ultimatum is repeated visits, made with no effort to buy anything. In a year or two you may establish cordial relations that will end in a purchase, or you may have all your calls for your pains.

For the past three summers an elderly farmer has kept an unusually fine Windsor chair on the porch of his house beside one of the main highways in New Hampshire. Automobile after automobile has stopped. The old man spends his days explaining that the chair is not for sale. Heart trouble holds him virtually a prisoner, but he is sociable. Unable to go to town and join in the talk at the general store, he has intentionally put this chair out where the world will see it and stop.

"What, sell my chair? No, siree. I'd be a mighty lonesome man without all the folks it brings me. It gives me something to do. In the winter I have to be satisfied with my radio, but from June to October my chair brings me all sorts and kinds of callers. I kept track last summer, and cars from all states but five pulled up before my place. I meet lots of different people. Sure, some get real mad when I won't sell; but then, I didn't ask them to stop, and the way they take on is downright amusing."

CHAPTER TWO

DETECTING THE GENUINE

ANTIQUE furniture can be judged by eye. Marks left by the old cabinetmaking tools, patina, grain of wood, structure, line, and other details are as recognizable to the experienced as the handwriting of a friend. Knowledge of them and detective skill in gathering such clues are part of the stock in trade of all seasoned buyers. Any piece can be made to testify whether it is real or fake and, with an observant buyer willing to accept the answers developed by deductive inspection, the chances of perjury are slight. An open mind is essential, for to start with a bias warps the judgment and makes it impossible for the eye to read the evidence aright.

A man who really knows his Early American furniture once completely duped himself by seeing what he wanted to see rather than what was there. At a farmhouse where he had just bought several old pine pieces he saw a gilt mirror hanging high up in the dusty dimness of the woodshed. He reached for it eagerly, accepting it as genuine before he could even get it down from its rusty nail. "I don't know what you want that for," came the honest voice of its owner. "It ain't my grandmother's or even my mother's. I got it ten years ago with a Larkin soap order." In line, this mirror was of the Federal period, and the collector's great desire for such a one momentarily blinded him to all indications of modern production. Only when the label, "Larkin & Co.," was firmly pointed out to him was he convinced.

Ability to recognize signs of old workmanship depends largely on understanding how the old cabinetmakers worked and what tools they used. Through the apprentice system their methods were so crystallized that nearly all Early American furniture has definite similarity in its fabrication. It was all produced by hand tools, and even the most careful workmen left tool marks that are clear and obvious.

At modern wage scales it costs too much to make copies by hand of any but the rarest pieces. Even then, at points which do not show, present-day shops cut corners by using machine-sawed and planed wood. The tracks of buzz saw and rotary plane are as legible as a highway advertising sign. Work done with them deceives only the unobservant and gullible. Likewise, not even the most carefully prepared stain can even approximate the patina which age, and age alone, imparts to the unvarnished surfaces of old wood. Undersides, backs, and interiors of old American furniture were always left raw. Dust and time have given them a tone that speaks for itself and defies imitation. Any piece which has stain, shellac, or varnish on its undersurfaces is open to suspicion. The chances are that it is either a reproduction or a reconstruction. True, an amateur, in his zeal to do thorough restoring to an old piece may have daubed raw wood surfaces inside and out. Generally, however, such work is not complete, and diligent search will uncover ample areas of time-stained raw wood. A chest of drawers which thirty years ago passed through the hands of a disciple of *The American Boy's Handy Book,* may have back boards and insides of drawers thoroughly stained or shellacked, but the interior of the case itself and the exterior of the drawers usually are untouched.

There is a whole category of crimes which, with paint and varnish, the youth of the nineties and early nineteen hundreds perpetrated on defenseless old furniture. In his Philistine past the author was as guilty as the rest. With spinal chills he remembers an especially heinous offense. It happened in the home of an indulgent aunt. He was one of a little group of nephews and nieces who were sure the furniture in the guest room would be improved by a nice coat of white enamel. So with righteous fervor and plenty of paint they advanced upon a Sheraton bureau, a field bed, some Windsor chairs, and other odd pieces. Not a square inch of mahogany, curly maple, or original Rhode Island green paint escaped. Even the brass drawer pulls made way for cheap cast glass knobs. When I remember the price paid years later to be rid of that same white paint, I wonder that my long-suffering relative ever let it happen; but indulgent elders in many families were accessories to crimes even worse than this.

One of Thomas Bailey Aldrich's nieces was allowed to cut off the legs of a graceful Queen Anne lowboy so that her room in the famous Nutter house in Portsmouth, New Hampshire, might have a dressing table approximating the popular princess mode.

The generation before the white enamel days also had their ideas about modernizing honest mahogany. To them skillful graining was the acme of elegance, and during the seventies and early eighties many pieces had their faces lifted by local painters who applied mustard-hued paints to simulate the look of black walnut or yellow oak. In short, each changing fashion in wood meant a coat of paint to many a good old piece. So look below the surface. Sheraton or Early Empire lines and a rosewood or black walnut finish simply means that some one tried to bring grandmother's old desk or chest of drawers up to date.

Whether a piece dates from the early Pilgrim years or the first quarter of the nineteenth century, one infallible indication of its genuineness is tool marks. When antiques were young, power-driven woodworking machinery was undreamt of. All parts were "worked up" by hand. After the lumber had been hand-sawed, an apprentice planed it to desired thinness with a heavy jack plane that left minute undulations on the surface. Our early cabinetmakers, being practical men, did not go further. Only that which showed was given added planing and scraping. Backs and undersurfaces were left as they came from the jack plane, which had a blade nearly three inches wide sharpened with a slight curve. All wood so planed has a surface covered with irregular ridges and hollows.

Look across such a piece toward the light, or pass the fingers over the surface lightly, and the track of the jack plane can be readily noted (*Illustration 4*). Traces of this tool are to be found on the back boards of desks, sideboards, and chests of drawers, the undersides of table tops and the soft wood frame of upholstered pieces. Four-post beds of the farmhouse type have these marks on side rails and back of the headboard.

Illustration 4. *(Home & Field from David J. Koser.)*

THE TRACK OF THE OLD JACK PLANE

This hand tool, because of the slight curve given the blade, left easily seen or felt ridges and hollows.

The saws used by the old workmen likewise left their trace. For coarse work ripsaws, worked vertically either by water power or by two men, left parallel straight scratches very different from the curved mark of the modern buzz saw (*Illustration 5*). Look for this tool track on the inside of table beds, the interior braces of desks and chests of drawers, and the back boards of such large pieces as corner cupboards, linen presses, and blanket chests.

Other common tool marks are scratches left by the scribing

awl, generally found where corners are dovetailed together, and chisel marks. Of the latter there are several kinds. That of the half-round gouging chisel, used to cut channels for screws,

A

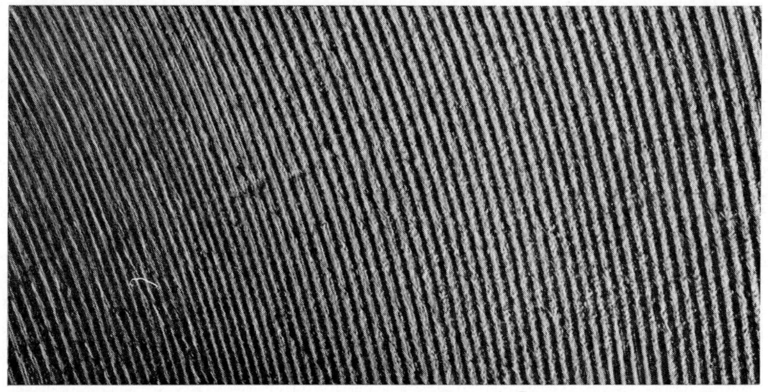

Illustration 5. *(Home & Field from David J. Koser)*

B

OLD AND NEW SAW MARKS COMPARED

A, Tooth marks of old ripsaws were straight. B, Those of a modern buzz saw are always arclike.

is found in various parts of sofas, along the frames of tables, and in desks and other pieces with shaped bracket feet. Its irregular cutting can be distinguished easily. In large pieces intended to be taken apart, such as four-post beds, the mark of the broad chisel used to cut mortises and tenons can be noticed (*Drawing 1*). Here the characteristic is the slight un-

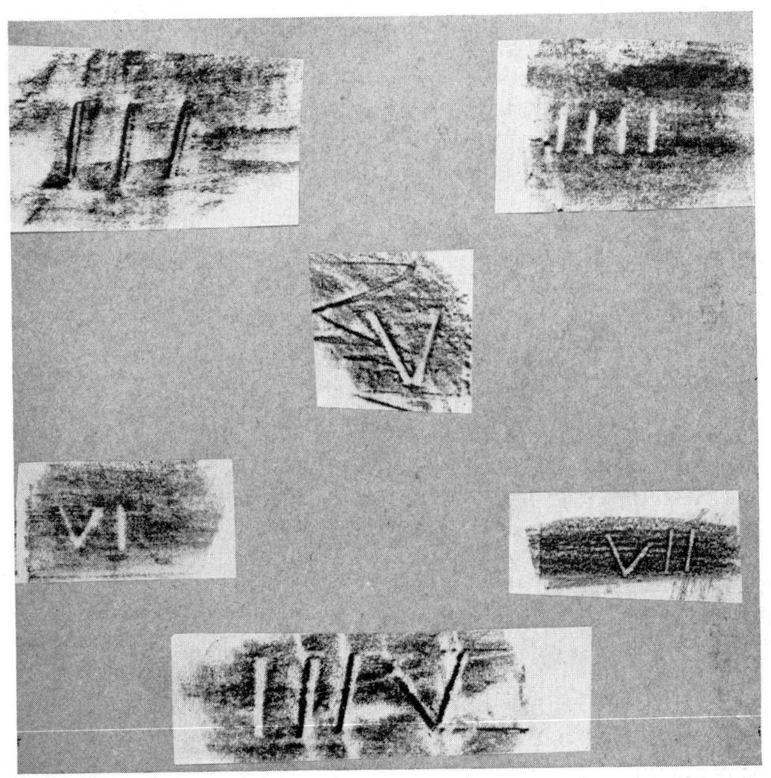

Drawing 1.

THE CHISEL NUMBERING HAD INDIVIDUALITY AKIN TO HANDWRITING

All parts of a piece should have like numbering. The number eight done backward was the work of a man unfamiliar with Roman numerals.

evenness common to all handwork. Such pieces also have their parts numbered in Roman numerals.

These numerals were fashioned with a flat chisel about half an inch wide, driven vertically into the wood about a sixteenth of an inch. A single vertical cut made the straight line for the one; two in a "v" formed the five and so forth. When a piece has numbered parts and these show distinctly that they were done by the same chisel and have corresponding idiosyncrasies of angle, they are the tool writing of one man and there is no doubt that all parts began life together. Bedposts and side rails are most commonly numbered, although such markings are found on both frame and seat of chairs with slip seats. These were often made in sets of six or more. Again, in some chests of drawers, chests on chests, and highboys, the drawers and drawer openings will be carefully numbered in this manner. Comparing them will tell the story whether it be of single origin or a job of assembling.

Dovetailing is another thing to be watched. Where drawer sides fit fronts and backs, flaring mortises and tenons were employed to make a firm joint. This was done also at the corners of square or rectangular frames such as the body of a chest of drawers. At times it was even used to fasten legs to the body of a piece. In the earliest dovetailing, found only for joints of box-form shapes, the dentation is not equal. It will alternate with one nearly two inches wide and then one not over an inch. Later these wedge-shaped teeth became nearer the same size. When they are exactly the same, workmanship of the early nineteenth century is indicated. A fancy scallop and very shallow work is the track of one of the early engine-driven woodworking machines.

On the other hand, some of the old cabinetmakers, such as the Rhode Island Townsends, had their own special variations of dovetail, and when known this is almost as good as an authentic label. To gain a working knowledge of old and modern dovetailing, study a number of drawer ends in some repair man's shop. If you are interested, he will rescue from his scrap pile samples that will show handwork as compared with that done by machines and may also be able to produce some of the older types of hand-done joints.

Where pieces have mortise-and-tenon joints held fast by small wooden pins, known as dowels, these should be studied closely, even with a pocket magnifying glass. The old dowels were made with plane, drawshave, and jackknife and so were never exactly round. Modern ones come from the machine mathematically circular. So perfectly round dowel ends indicate that the piece either has been completely taken apart and new dowels used in re-assembling or is modern work.

Along with tool marks, tone of the patina should be taken into consideration. Here again the out-of-sight parts, which the old craftsmen never stained or varnished, will tell the story. Time and dust give unfinished wood a mellow tone varying from a golden brown for the soft woods and maple to a copper-red for birch, cherry, and old red walnut. Time-aged and unvarnished mahogany is lighter and grayer than the varnished surfaces of the same wood. If studied in bright sunlight the patina of old, unfinished wood will have a bloom while that of new wood stained to simulate age will have a dull, dirty look. Once observed, this difference can never be mistaken. Also, it is well to remember that the varnished parts of an old piece, even when carefully scraped and refinished, will be somewhat darker than new wood of the same variety. Attempts to simulate this by adding stains and dyes to new wood result only in a dirty tone.

Notice the wood or combination of wood from which a piece was made. Remember that what is known as three-ply veneer is a modern invention. Drawer bottoms, bed headboards, and the like were never made of such material. Likewise, chair legs, seats for Windsor chairs, and bedposts were always fashioned from single pieces of lumber. The practice of using "built-up" material, made by gluing several pieces together to get the desired width or thickness, is a sure sign of new workmanship.

Old bedposts were turned from lumber three to six inches square and often have vertical cracks due to gradual seasoning over the years. Such cracks are most often found on the simpler farmhouse type of beds. Here the posts and side rails may be of maple, yellow birch, cherry, beech, or walnut while the headboard will be of pine or other soft wood. This was a general practice although for particularly nice beds the wood of all parts was the same.

When antique furniture was being made, there were vogues in wood and style structure just as now. The 17th Century used oak for fine pieces and pine or other soft wood at hand for ordinary furnishings. This furniture was of simple structure. Wainscot paneling formed the sides, and ornamentation was achieved by shallow carving. Geometric or conventional flower patterns were used. The William and Mary and Queen Anne periods brought in native hard woods such as maple, birch, walnut, and sometimes cherry. The structure was less primitive, and bird's-eye and curly maple began to be used. Burl or crotch walnut veneer was also in favor for decorative fronts, particularly during the William and Mary years. In fact, woods with irregular grain so captured the public taste that village cabinetmakers continued their use until furniture making was transferred to factories.

With the Chippendale influence, mahogany made its appearance and rapidly supplanted all other materials for the finer furniture. Rural craftsmen still used the native hard woods, however, and even worked in apple and pear wood. The combination of mahogany and native fancy grained woods was a marked characteristic of the American Hepplewhite and Sheraton styles. Many pieces were made in which a mahogany framework and bird's-eye or curly maple parts were combined most effectively.

Then came the American Empire, characterized at the last by great bulk and little grace; the use of native woods declined; rosewood was introduced about 1825, and last of all came a dark-hued wood aptly called black walnut to distinguish it from the reddish variety that had been used since the beginning of the 18th Century.

The nationality of antique furniture can to a degree be determined by structural characteristics. American pieces are sturdier. Each element is heavier, and where there is carving it is never so deep or elaborate as in English or Continental

Illustration 6. *(Museum of Fine Arts, Boston)*

AN ENGLISH CHINESE CHIPPENDALE TABLE

Carving as elaborate as this is not characteristic of American pieces. Sir William Chambers published his book of Chinese studies in 1757. This initiated the Chinese conceit that Chippendale frequently employed.

pieces (*Illustration 6*). Drawers, back boards, and interior parts of imported antiques are made largely of oak. American workmen used either pine or spruce. With chests of drawers, English and European craftsmen had a refinement seldom practiced by even our best cabinetmakers. They built their chests with wide boards which completely separated each drawer from the one above or beneath. Known as dust boards, these are nearly always a sign of foreign birth. Then there is the wood beneath the veneers. Our workmen used soft woods while Europeans employed oak or poorer qualities of the same wood as the veneer itself.

Normal signs of wear are a great aid in judging antique furniture. Remember, a genuine antique must have seen at least a century of use. Years of dusting have dulled the glaze of original varnish on even prized pieces kept in the seldom-used parlor. The battle scars of those in everyday use are most apparent. All sharp edges are dulled; tops have been stained by liquids or marred by overheated dishes; feet and legs are dented and scratched, particularly near the floor (*Illustration 7*). In desks and chests of drawers, evidence of long use is in the lower edges of the drawer sides. It is on these that the drawer moves, sliding on runners glued or nailed to the framework. In extreme cases drawer sides will be found worn down half an inch, and the runners may have grooves a quarter of an inch deep.

Study chair legs and cross members for marks of wear. Years of use will have left their traces. The lower ends of the legs will be polished by a century or more of rubbing along floors. Above, there will be fine little dents, bruises, and scratches beyond the power of the faker to imitate. Notice the cross stretchers. Years of catching heels will have left their mark. The upper side of rungs may be worn almost flat, and where the horizontals are four-sided the upper edge will be distinctly worn away. Heel-wear applied artificially is overdone. It is too uniform and has an intentional pattern not hard to recognize. Slat-back chairs have their own special sign of wear.

Illustration 7. *(Dr. George P. Coopernail)*

NORMAL SIGNS OF WEAR

On the raised lid of this Hepplewhite card table that dates from 1790–1810, can be seen circles left by moist glasses and hot dishes as well as the fine scratches made by particles of grit in dusting.

Illustration 8. *(Author's collection)*

AN 18TH CENTURY READING LIGHT

Slat-back chair with iron candlesticks hung on upper slats. The flames of these often charred the finials. Nearness to floor of front and rear rungs shows that the legs have been cut off. This chair was made sometime during the latter half of the 18th Century and taken from southern New England to Vermont before 1800.

Burns and charred spots are frequently found along the upper slat and finials of the back. Before the advent of the whale-oil lamp it was a common custom to hang small wrought-iron candlesticks on the upper rail. With lighted candles thus attached over right and left shoulder, one could read with fair ease. This was practical but unsafe, as the candles were apt to burn irregularly and scorch the chair (*Illustration 8*). Candlesticks for this use were made with a special lip at the top to hook over the chair slat and were usually long enough for the base to rest against the second slat—obviously an unstable arrangement: more than one grandsire had to interrupt his reading to put out an incipient fire. In his *Story of a Bad Boy,* Thomas Bailey Aldrich makes much of the way Grandfather Nutter would sedately extinguish such blazes and then, unruffled, return to his reading.

Along with indications of use, hardware, nails, and screws should be inspected. For a piece to come through years of service with its brasses intact is remarkable and adds distinctly to its value. If original, they will be of the period of the piece and the drawer fronts will have no other holes bored in them than those for these brasses. If screws and nails are also original, they will be hand-wrought. Machine-made ones date from about 1840, and a piece put together entirely with them either dates accordingly or has been rebuilt (*Illustration 9*).

Beyond rebuilding, there is the practice of too generous restoration known as glorifying. Some of the tricks of the glorifier are: additions of inlay and carving to plain pieces, substitution of parts from other pieces, and mismating. This last includes such things as assembling four-post beds from stray parts, cutting over tops or bases of highboys so they will match, and equipping a simple secretary with a stray bookcase top. Where this has been done, the carving will be too sharp, and details and proportions will vary enough to show that the piece is assembled and not original.

Any well-informed buyer recognizes when a piece has been altered by the addition of parts or decorations belonging to another period. Sometimes the alteration has been intentional and sometimes through ignorance. The result is the same. Chippendale proportions and outline do not go with Empire carving. Leaded glass does not belong in the doors of secretaries dating around 1770, but rather wooden panels.

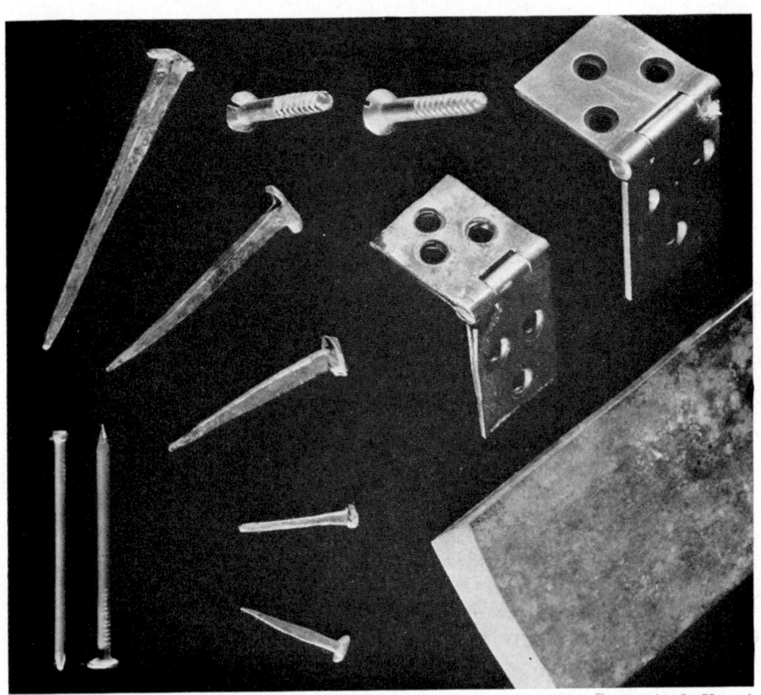

Illustration 9. *(Home & Field from David J. Koser)*

OLD AND MODERN SCREWS, NAILS, AND HINGES

The irregularities of handwork are readily observed as well as the regularity of modern machine products. At lower right hand is the blade of an old plane with its curved edge.

Such mismating and adapting is usually the work of an uninformed and not too scrupulous dealer, but sometimes it took place many years ago with no intention to defraud. In a Connecticut village a surgeon, an ardent collector by avocation, found a highboy base which was offered to him as a lowboy. It was too tall for a regulation lowboy, and he recognized it as the base of a highboy which had been converted long ago by adding a top board. Instead of scorning the piece, which was a Queen Anne of excellent line, he questioned its owner and so found the upper section in her sister's home ten miles away. Both were elderly women. The piece had originally belonged to their grandmother. The Empire feet which converted the top into a chest of drawers showed that this particular bit of adapting had been done in her time. It cost this surgeon several trips and much diplomacy to induce the other sister to sell. At first she would not believe the two pieces were originally one. Finally, by a demonstration in which top and bottom were shorn of their additions, he won the day.

Dealers and collectors who like to buy their antiques in their original locations have another danger against which they must be on guard. That is the misinformation and cock-and-bull stories which owners will tell. Quite innocently such people will tell the most astounding lies. Family tradition is most unreliable. As time goes on, pieces get fifty and a hundred years added to their age, and the present owner believes what he is telling implicitly. To doubt is to question the integrity of an honest person and somehow besmirch family honor. Worst of all, it is apt to develop hostility and make buying impossible. In such circumstances a wise buyer lets the seller talk uncontradicted. If the piece coincides with its ascribed history and antiquity, so much the better. If not, he accepts what the piece itself tells him and does not try to correct the owner's story.

Years ago I lost a nice set of Windsor chairs that could have been mine for nothing if only I had held my tongue. They belonged to an older cousin who had helped raise me. Unused, these chairs were in her attic and when I admired them she said I might have them. Then she started to tell me that they had belonged to our Revolutionary great-great-grandmother and had been brought from Rhode Island about 1790. The chairs were unmistakably Windsors of the 1820 type and—I contradicted Cousin Elizabeth. Was she mad! Would she let a boy young enough to be her son tell her she lied? No, if they were such poor things as I said they were, she would not give them to anyone. The gift was revoked and never, never afterward could I mention these Windsor without calling forth a fresh burst of wrath. Later they went to a more tactful cousin who had the good sense not to disagree. He knew that they were made for the son of the Revolutionary ancestor and had never even been out of their native Vermont, but he held his peace and got the chairs.

If normal signs of wear offer corroborating testimony to genuineness, abnormal and artificial signs speak just as loudly of faking. When the counterfeiter tries to make his product look old by applying wear-marks, he generally overdoes it or puts them in the wrong place. We have all heard of the man whose trade is boring wormholes in near-antiques. He is supposed to have skill beyond detection, but expert testimony in a court action once threw a new light on this. An antique specialist in the United States Customs Service took the stand and staged a simple demonstration. He put broom splints into the "wormholes" of the piece under question and showed the jury how each stood upright. This proved they were man-made, since real wormholes always follow the grain of the wood and run at all angles imaginable.

The newest wrinkle of the out-and-out antique faker is the counterfeit label. Forged labels bearing the names of several of the best American cabinetmakers of the Chippendale period are now in circulation (*Illustration 10*). Fortunately, they are not well enough executed to defy detection. If one is considering purchase of a piece bearing a label of a well-known cabinetmaker and is not already familiar with the design and typography of authenticated examples of his label, careful comparison is a wise precaution. There are several antique furniture books that include among their illustrations photographs of the real labels used by these men. There is such wide variance between a genuine and a spurious label that an expert on typography and engraving will not be needed. Also do not feel that the dealer will be insulted because you wish to make this investigation. Any reputable one will respect your thoroughness and put his reference books at your dis-

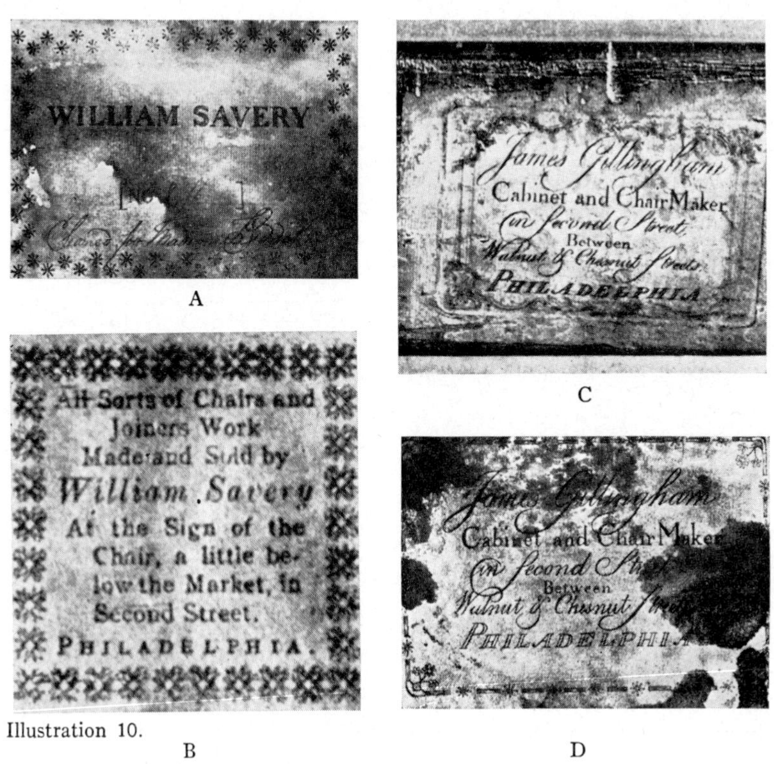

Illustration 10.

GENUINE VERSUS FORGED LABELS

Defects of design and lettering make it possible to recognize forged labels. A, Savery counterfeit. B, Genuine Savery. C, Gillingham counterfeit. D, Genuine Gillingham.

posal. Thorough investigation never lessens the value of a genuine piece, labeled or not, nor reduces the chances of a sale.

Almost in the same class with the spurious label is the use of a newspaper advertisement of certain old cabinetmakers clipped from a paper of the period and pasted into an unlabeled

Glaſſes, &c.

¶ THOMAS HEWES,
UPHOLSTERER,
In Cheſtnut-ſtreet, near Second-ſtreet, PHILADELPHIA,

MAKES all Sorts of UPHOLSTERERS WORK, in the neateſt and neweſt Faſhions, at the moſt reaſonable Prices, ſuch as Beds and Window Curtains, Eaſy Chairs, Couches, Matraſſes, either of Hair or Wool, Feather Beds, Sacking Bottoms, Chair Bottoms and Ship Stools, &c. &c.

THOSE that are pleaſed to favour him with their CUSTOM, may depend on CARE and DISPATCH. Tbc. 6 W.

On the 21ſt Day of this inſtant December, will be expoſed to

Illustration 11.

A CLIPPING, NOT A LABEL

Old newspaper advertising is sometimes attached to a piece to simulate a label. Lack of margins, typography, and absence of a border framing the words betray the deception.

piece. These can be identified in two ways (*Illustration 11*): First, the clipping reads like an advertisement and not a label; second, there is an insufficient border of white paper around the type, and sometimes even the column rules can be seen.

Such are the main points to be observed in judging old furniture. Willingness to examine pieces carefully, a keen eye, and practice, these three, and the greatest of these is practice.

CHAPTER THREE

OUR CABINETMAKERS—WHERE AND HOW THEY WORKED

FURNITURE making in America seems to have prospered from the start. The reason is not difficult to find. Compared with the meanest of tramp freighters today, the ships which brought the colonists were mere cockleshells. One hundred and fifty tons burden was a large boat in the colonial years. Consequently cargo space was so limited that the early colonists could bring little of a furniture nature beyond the plainest of trunklike chests. The only surviving piece that can be said beyond question to have come over in the *Mayflower,* is Peregrine White's wicker cradle, a prophetic emblem of the new colony.

As to the legion of other pieces reputed to have emigrated on that hundred-ton boat, careful examination has almost invariably proved them to be fabricated of woods found only in the New World. There is a distinct difference in texture between English and American oak as well as other woods. So, many pieces once thought to have come from the old country have been found with an American accent in their wood. The Elder Brewster and the Governor Winthrop chairs, imposing archiepiscopal seats for important personages, come under this category.

If there was no room to bring household furnishings, some one had to make them in the new land. Fine wood for making tables and chairs, beds and chests, was to be had for the cutting. Accordingly, Americans went to making furniture about as soon as they had roofs over their heads. Cabinetmakers were among the early arrivals, and they established the furniture-making proclivities of the colonies.

What the 17th Century produced in the northern colonies is fairly well known. In the South we have to depend on wills and inventories to gain any idea of the furniture, since practically no piece antedating 1700 has survived. However, these documents show that the planters' homes were well supplied with pieces appraised at sizable amounts in pounds of tobacco, the medium of exchange of the day. In all probability they were locally made. By the second quarter of the 18th Century, however, the southern colonies had become so completely agricultural, with slave labor bearing the brunt of the toil, that less and less furniture was made each year. Some of the great plantations had their negro cabinetmakers, trained under indentured servants from England, and some towns such as Charleston, South Carolina, had their groups of cabinetmakers ready to supply local wants. Both were, in the main, exceptions rather than the rule. Recent researches indicate more southern furniture making than has heretofore been conceded. The lively coastal shipping that brought salt fish and other commodities from the more industrial North also carried a great deal of furniture, and this of course was copied by the southern craftsmen just as those of New England used English pieces and books of design for their inspiration. The outcome of this was furniture basically northern with southern variations.

Of course men of great wealth like Washington might and did order furniture from their London factors, but there were comparatively few Washingtons. The majority depended on what they could buy locally from the captains of coastwise sailing vessels. It was this trade that provided many of the furnishings used on the manor farms of Delaware and Maryland and the plantations of Virginia and the Carolinas.

Recollections of pieces as New England as a Salem doorway seen in the South once spurred me to investigate, and I found that our early cabinetmakers, as well as those who were active during the Empire period, had well-established methods for disposing of their output in distant localities. 18th and early

19th Century newspapers, from the first issue of the Boston *News Letter,* reveal an impressive volume of coastwise shipping.

From Maine to Georgia and all through the West Indies the sloops, brigs, and schooners of northern ports bore varied cargoes, which, besides such merchandise as dried fish and negro shoes, included more furniture than is generally realized. At first these furniture shipments were individual enterprises. A cabinetmaker in a port town—and virtually every coastal village with a harbor was, in those days, a shipping centre—might have on hand a larger stock than he could hope to sell locally. In such cases he would arrange with a friendly skipper to transport this excess on a forthcoming trade voyage. Colonial ship captains were more than navigators. They were seagoing business men. A large part of their cargoes represented consignments that it was their task to sell as advantageously as possible at various ports of call. The proceeds of such sales would be in part invested in return cargo, in part held in cash. When a ship reached home, her captain settled with his consignors, and then divided his profits with the vessel's owners.

About 1800, a new factor appeared in the furniture trade. This was the man who bought excess production directly from cabinetmakers and chairmakers for speculative purposes. His business was to gather new furniture where it was plentiful, and relatively cheap, and ship it to localities where it would bring good prices. Such men were known as shippers. They continued their activities until about 1850. Toward the close of this era, their principal markets were the West Indies and Latin America; but before that they also did much business in the South.

The earliest definite record that I have found of the southward shipping of New England furniture deals with Ipswich-made pieces marketed in Maryland and Virginia. Thomas Franklin Waters, in his book *Ipswich in the Massachusetts Bay Colony,* cites two examples of this commerce quoted from account books and correspondence. The first concerns a voyage to Maryland and Virginia made, in the fall of 1786, by the *Hannah,* forty-five tons, William Gray, Jr., master. The cargo, which consisted exclusively of commodities made at Ipswich, included twelve desks, six tables, and four dozen chairs. The unsold surplus was left with George Blackwell, Virginia agent. His receipt, naming the cabinetmaking consignors and listing individual pieces with their value in pounds, shillings, and pence, is as follows:

	1 desk with secret Drawers & glass in ye front	£2:17:4
Nathaniel Lord	1 desk	2:17:4
Elisha Newman	1 desk	2:17:4
Abraham Knowlton	3 desks	8:12:6
William Appleton	1 desk	2:17:4
Daniel Lummus	1 table	8:0
Joseph Lord	1 table	6:0
Daniel Lummus	6 white chairs at 14; Daniel Smith	
Daniel Lord	6 chairs at 3	5:20

On the basis of the prices recorded in this receipt, the total value of the furniture borne by the *Hannah* on this voyage was approximately twenty-five pounds, a tidy sum for the Ipswich craftsmen. The "white chairs" were not painted white; the term indicated unfinished wood. Mr. Waters tells of another shipment of Ipswich furniture consigned to Moses Taylor in Virginia. Writing back to Ipswich, Taylor reports that he is still holding for sale:

Nathaniel Lord	3 chairs, 2 large tables and a small one valued 4/3 and a desk	£ 2:0:0
Joseph Lord	a desk	2:10:0
William Appleton	a small desk	1:0:0
Jeremiah Kimball	2 large oval tables	2:2:0
John Ringe	2 tables	0:8:0
Moses Lord	chairs	0:15:0
Daniel Smith	8 chairs	0:16:0
Daniel Smith	6 white chairs	0:12:0

It is easy to calculate that, at this time—between 1786 and 1790—the market value of desks was two pounds ten shillings, small desks one pound, large oval tables one pound one shilling, ordinary tables four shillings, and chairs two shillings each. The questions that naturally arise are, What became of this furniture of Ipswich origin? and How much of it is now credited to Maryland or Virginia craftsmen? Other records of similar shipments from New England centres before 1800 are to be found in local histories and shipping records. The listed destinations include Savannah, Charleston, Wilmington (North Carolina), and various places in Maryland and Virginia.

Just who were the individuals who carried on business as furniture shippers, we may never know. But an advertisement of Nolen & Gridley, auctioneers, in the Boston *Columbian Centinel,* February 16, 1811, indicates that those speculative gentlemen were considered well worth cultivating. The advertisement reads:

CHAIRS AND CABINET FURNITURE FOR SHIPPING

Nolen & Gridley have for sale, at their ware room, Nos. 27 and 28 Cornhill—3,000 Chairs, comprising a very complete assortment, from the best workmanship, and finest touch of the pencil, to the most common, from 70 to 6 dlls. per doz. all which they will pack in shipping order, and in the most careful manner; Secretaries, side Boards; Bureaus; light and wash Stands; night cabinets; dining, Pembroke, and card Tables; Ladies' work Stands; 100 portable desks; 50 bedsteads etc. All orders for Furniture for shipping to suit any market, either in the Cabinet or Chair line, of any description, may be had, at the shortest notice by applying at the above Warehouse.

N.B. Town and Country Customers may be supplied with the best work at such prices as cannot fail of giving satisfaction to purchasers. Gentlemen and ladies are respectfully invited to call and see for themselves.

Just a few days prior to this announcement there appeared in the same paper another advertisement that seems to indicate the origin of a part, at least, of the Nolen & Gridley stock. It is an announcement to the effect that the warden of the state prison at Charlestown will sell at auction a large quantity of furniture made by the inmates of his institution. The list of items offered is so similar to that published by Nolen & Gridley as to suggest that the latter were liberal purchasers at the prison sale.

Traveling south from Boston and consulting the newspapers as we go, we shall find evidence of the jobber and his methods. For instance, in the New York *Evening Post* for May 11, 1817, McGraw & Company advertise:

> Cabinet Makers and Piano Forte Makers—Those having dead stock on hand and who are desirous to make advantageous sales are invited to a confidential arrangement with McGraw & Co., Masonic Temple, where liberal advances will be made, and Great facilities offered. Shippers supplied with furniture suitable for any market.

Another New York advertisement, that of a cabinetmaker bidding directly for the shippers' trade, is that of Wheaton and Davis, which, for some months during 1819, appeared in the *Evening Post*. It reads:

> Fancy and Mahogany Chair & Sofa Manufactory.
> 156 Fulton Street opposite St. Paul's Church.
> Wheaton and Davis respectfully inform the public that they have for sale a large and elegant assortment of mahogany, curled maple, rosewood and fancy painted chairs, sofas etc. richly ornamented in gold and bronze with hair, cane and rush seats. Shippers orders for any part of the continent executed with dispatch.

Deming & Bulkley, Robert Kelly, and many others were among the New York cabinetmakers who from time to time advertised that they were ready to supply furniture to shippers. Deming & Bulkley apparently did some distant wholesale marketing on their own account, for the Charleston directories for 1829 and 1831 carry the listing "Deming & Bulkley, furniture warehouse, 218 King Street." Robert Kelly, on the other hand, in his advertising emphasizes the fact that he "warrants to be manufactured of the best materials and workmanship such as to stand the southern climate." It will, perhaps, likewise be recalled that Duncan Phyfe's brother Lachlan is listed in Baltimore directories, 1807 to 1809. He may have been agent for the New York shop. That Phyfe had other agents in the South seems probable. In this connection it is worthy of note that of the three known pieces of furniture bearing Duncan Phyfe's label one was found in Georgia.

How far these New York cabinetmakers or their shippers sent their furniture is indicated by the inventory of the estate of the French *ébéniste* Lannuier, who had a shop at 60 Broad Street from about 1805 to 1819. In this inventory occur two illuminating entries:

Furniture sent to A. S. Bullock of Savannah,	$2,401.25
Furniture to Trinidad de Cuba, consigned to Capt Roy,	534.00

Again, in the only advertisement of William M. Tweed, the famous boss of the unsavory Tweed Ring, we read "fine gilt and variegated colored Chairs, a large assortment boxed suitable for the Spanish & West Indian markets."

New York and New England by no means enjoyed a monoply in catering to distant consumers. In Philadelphia we find auctioneers and craftsmen alike advertising their willingness to provide extensive lines of furniture properly built to stand the ravages of coastal trade and southern climate. Among these announcements are those of Gridley & Co., auctioneers, Thomas Welch, cabinetmaker, Johan Fuches, chairmaker, and a number of others.

Baltimore cabinetmakers may have also cultivated the enterprising shipper. Thus far I have found no advertisement to support such a surmise, though Dr. Berkley, in his *Register of Cabinet Makers,* gives a quite formidable list of Baltimore sales houses and importers of furniture from 1777 to 1820. In any case it is of little moment whether Baltimore or Philadelphia was the southern limit for furniture shipping. We know that to the northward the trade was well established, and that during some seventy-five years it was carried on with sufficient vigor to account for all the Yankee pieces that have been found below the Mason and Dixon line—and many more yet to be discovered.

Just as the old cabinetmakers had well established channels of distribution that carried their products far and wide, there were others that provided them with supplies not produced locally. The trade in mahogany grew to be more and more of a specialty as the wood gained general acceptance. By 1800 and even before, it was divorced from the general lumber trade in the principal centres, and "Mahogany yard" was such a standard classification in both early directories and newspaper advertising as to make it quite evident that handling this wood in timbers, planks, and boards was a recognized trade of itself. Some of the cabinetmakers leased the space behind their shops for such yards—a canny move which placed a good assortment of cabinet wood right at their back doors. Others, like Duncan Phyfe, maintained their own yards. Beginning about 1815, he had one of the second generation of his family at the head of a subsidiary yard of this type at 39 Harrison Street for a number of years.

For mirrors, shaving glasses, and sconces, the city cabinetmakers seem to have depended on importations rather than on their own production. This accounts for many mirrors with delicate frames and characteristically English execution that are found in old family collections where the rest of the furniture is distinctly American in fabrication. Similarly, the dainty shaving and dressing table glasses with shield-shaped frame, curved supports, and miniature cabinet with small drawers beneath, speak distinctly of English make even though some bear labels of American dealers (*Illustration 12*).

These pieces were novelties and of small size that made it better business to import them than to produce them at home. Mirror-making as a branch of cabinetwork, except for the crude 17th Century efforts, does not seem to have come into being here until after the Chippendale years. Then a

Illustration 12. *(Ginsburg & Levy, Inc.)*

AN ENGLISH HEPPLEWHITE SHAVING MIRROR

Made about 1785. Pieces of this sort were imported and widely sold in America. Few were of native make. Even when such a piece bears an American label, it is generally that of the importer.

Illustration 13. *(American Art Assn.–Anderson Galleries)*

A GILT MIRROR OF AMERICAN MAKE

The naval battle scene shown in the upper panel dates this just after the close of the War of 1812.

Illustration 14.

TYPICAL AMERICAN CHIPPENDALE MIRROR

The wood is mahogany. Made about 1760–1770.

number of craftsmen produced gilded framed glasses with or without a pictorial panel at the top. Among the better known whose labeled pieces have been located, were Peter Grinnell and Son, Providence; Hobbs & Jenkins, Boston, who styled their business "ornament manufactory"; several firms using various combinations of the name Cermenati and another Italian surname, all located in New England; Kidder and Carter, Charlestown, Massachusetts, and Charles Del Vecchio of New York (*Illustration 13*).

In the Chippendale period there was John Elliot in Philadelphia, whose label was printed both in English and in German to fit the particular business situation there (*Illustration 14*). I do not think he produced the better mirrors so marked; rather he imported them. For instance, one of his newspaper advertisements begins:

> Just imported in the Mary and Elizabeth, Captain Sparks and other vessels from London . . . A very large, neat and genteel assortment of looking glasses.

And so on through a long list of sconce, pier and over-mantel mirrors. It is illustrated with a shaving glass distinctly of English work. His advertisement shows how the Pre-Revolutionary mirrors of the best types of Queen Anne and Chippendale design reached America, and I think this also holds true of those done in the Hepplewhite and Sheraton modes. He also offers to resilver and reframe old glasses, so it is evident that he combined importing with domestic production and repair work.

The cruder of the 18th Century mirrors were undoubtedly made in America as were many of those of the 19th Century that carried patriotic scenes or emblems in the upper panel and, towards the last, conventionalized fruit and flower designs or simple landscapes that in a way heralded the coming of the Currier & Ives lithographs (*Illustration 15*).

The labels and advertising of some of the looking-glass men also give us an indication of the source of the brass hardware

Illustration 15. *(Dr. George P. Coopernail)*

A B C

A, Early 18th Century. B and C, Empire, about 1825.
SIMPLE AMERICAN MIRRORS

used on chests of drawers, desks, and the like. They speak of their assortment of imported cabinet brasswares. While the furniture craftsmen may have turned to local blacksmiths for wrought-iron hinges, nails, screws, and simpler locks, their brasses were from the old country. The brass founders of England then as now made a superior product. Until Paul Revere forsook silversmithing for copper and its alloys, practically no trace can be found of this craft in America.

The English Parliament, always prone to protect home industries at the expense of its colonials, saw to that. Colonial brass founding was specifically forbidden by the legislators of Westminster. On the other hand, English producers of cabinet brasses cultivated the American trade both before and after the Revolution most assiduously. They issued elaborate catalogues in which their products were depicted most carefully, style by style. Copper-plate engravings were used, and each handle, escutcheon, finial, hinge, or bracket shown bore its identifying number. The mail-order idea, a century before Sears Roebuck or Montgomery Ward!

Several of these English hardware catalogues are in the library of the Essex Institute. The watermarks in the paper prove English origin and, in some, 18th Century publication. That is all. No name, not a line of descriptive text, and no prices. Who issued them and what prices were quoted were matters to be covered in private correspondence. Hence it was perfectly safe for a cabinetmaker to show his customers these style books. They could not glean from them any trade secrets.

Appropriate brasses for a style continued to be made long after it had been superseded by another. One of these catalogues, published in 1790, shows the simple tear drops of the William and Mary; the engraved or chased brasses with drop handles of the Queen Anne; the Chippendale bail and plate drawer pulls, going through many variations of what was a conventionalized bird with outspread wings. Then there were the oval and round brasses of Hepplewhite that in some cases

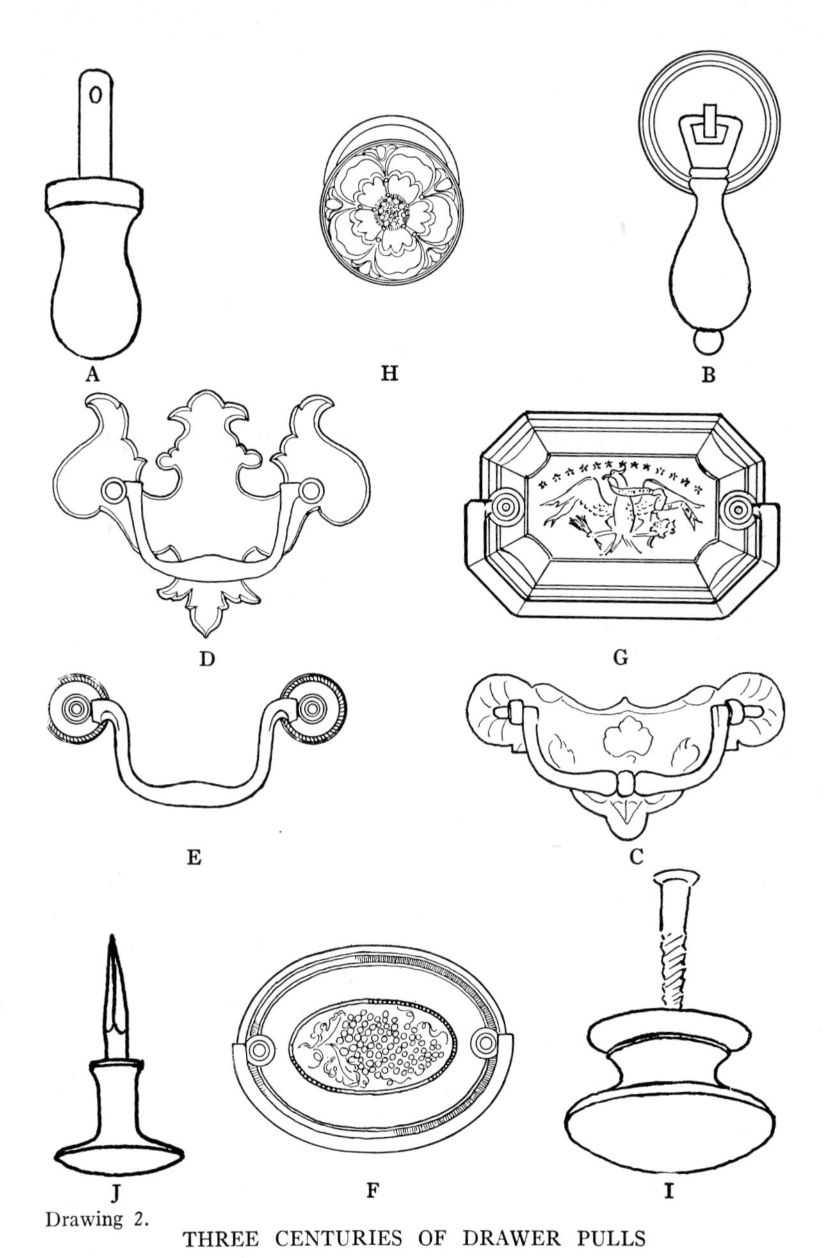

Drawing 2.

THREE CENTURIES OF DRAWER PULLS

A, wooden knob of the 17th Century; B, William and Mary brass tear drop; C, engraved brass of Queen Anne period with bail handle; D and E, Chippendale developments of this type; F and G, types used with Hepplewhite and Sheraton pieces; H, gilded brass knob of the Early Empire; I, wooden knob of the latter Empire years; J, small brass knob used for top supports and small interior drawers of desks and secretaries.

carried a design of American appeal in stamped relief, such as a coat-of-arms eagle with shield, stars and, in its claws, the arrows of war and the olive branch of peace (*Drawing* 2).

In addition, a great many styles were depicted of small knobs for desk interiors, simple and specialized types of hinges, finials of the ball and spire variety, eagles in full flight, and locks and keys. Clockmakers, too, were not forgotten. For them, hands, dials, and (breathe it softly) movement parts semi-finished which only needed a final filing before being assembled as American-made timepieces.

Whether English workmen also produced the inlays used by American cabinetmakers cannot be proved by a convenient picture book like those of the brass founders. There is enough similarity of design to make it a reasonable supposition. We do know that inlay medallions were made in block form about two inches thick and then cut off as wanted much as we slice a boiled ham. The more intricate moldings were also made thus while the simpler, narrow ones of two or three thicknesses of woods of contrasting colors were probably produced by the individual craftsmen in their own shops.

But while such accessories were imported, the bulk of the furnishings for the Early American home was made not only in this country but by men working north of Chesapeake Bay. The data in the United States census of 1810—the first one in which information on industries and their production was gathered—corroborate this. Its tabulations show conclusively that cabinetmaking was primarily a northern occupation.

And who were the cabinetmakers of the North? Probably John Speak-for-Yourself Alden was the first. After him came many whose names and occupations are mentioned in early records, but Nicholas Disbrowe of Hartford, Connecticut, is the earliest whose identified work still survives. His carved oaken chest marked "Mary Allyn's chist cutte and joyned by Nich. Disbrowe," now owned by Luke Vincent Lockwood, is the earliest piece of American furniture for which the maker can be given. Disbrowe worked in Hartford from 1639 to

1683. Then there is a gap of over half a century. The men who made the William and Mary and Queen Anne furniture are still shrouded in the oblivion that covered all the Early American cabinetmakers before the turn of the 20th Century.

Suddenly in Rhode Island and Philadelphia there arose two groups of masters whose identity and identified pieces are now well established. At Newport there was the Townsend-Goddard dynasty comprised of Job and Christopher Townsend, 1700–1765; John Goddard, son-in-law of Job, 1723–1785, and John Townsend, son of Christopher, 1730–1800. This group began working in the Queen Anne style, shifted to the Chippendale, and then concluded by making some remarkably fine Hepplewhite pieces. In Massachusetts, during the latter part of their reign they had as contemporaries, Benjamin Frothingham, Abner Toppan, and several lesser men.

In Philadelphia the gifted disciples of that English master furniture designer, Thomas Chippendale, included William Savery, 1721–1787; Jonathan Gostelowe, 1744–1795; Benjamin Randolph, 1762–1792. In the more or less neighboring city of New Brunswick, New Jersey, this group had a distinguished contemporary, Matthew Egerton, 1739–1802. Recent indications are that there were several craftsmen of first rank in New York but sufficient proven samples of their work have not yet been discovered to warrant listing them.

But with the advent of the United States as now constituted, New York took the lead by virtue of Duncan Phyfe, 1768–1854, whose brilliant early work for some years crowded out of consideration any of his contemporaries in that city or elsewhere. Now, however, we know that they included Samuel McIntire, the Salem cabinetmaker and carver, 1757–1811; Henry Connelly of Philadelphia, 1770–1826; Matthew Egerton, Jr.; Mills & Deming, a New York partnership that produced very fine Hepplewhite sideboards about 1790; Robert Lawton, also a New York disciple of Hepplewhite, who worked at about the same time; Joseph Rawson & Son, Providence, Rhode Island, 1790–1800; John Seymour and Son of Boston, 1800–1810, whose standing rests on one unusually fine secretary that sold a few years back for $30,000 and Honoré Lannuier, the Frenchman, who worked in New York from 1805 until 1819. There were others, but they were lesser men; and as this is not a check list of the known cabinetmakers, we will pass them by along with the chairmakers and those who produced the banjo and Yankee clocks.

Before Phyfe retired, factory-made furniture had begun to spread its blight across the land. The individuality of the craftsman was gone, and with it the excellence of work that makes it worth collecting. In the good old days furniture making was a personal matter. The masters worked at the bench themselves and wrought their wares slowly and thoroughly. If their trade was flourishing, they had journeymen and apprentices who worked under them—Phyfe had a hundred—but what was turned out in any shop bore the unmistakable imprint of the master at the head. For designs at first, these workmen had what they remembered of the style in vogue in England before they left. Such are known as memory pieces, and in their design and execution can be seen a distinct mingling of the old with new ideas developed in the New World.

How the William and Mary and Queen Anne styles reached America is not clear. Probably they were brought by lately arrived journeymen who may have had some sketches wrapped with their tools. With Chippendale it was different. In 1754 he published his book of designs *The Gentleman & Cabinet-maker's Director,* and we know that copies of it were in the hands of a number of the American cabinetmakers. The same applies to Hepplewhite's book issued in 1788 and the series of books that Thomas Sheraton produced.

These books were not production blueprints, but sketches from which craftsmen could get suggestions and inspiration for their own work. How well they functioned is proved by the fine examples of Chippendale, Hepplewhite, and Sheraton

A

Illustration 16.

B

AMERICAN CHAIRS COMPARED WITH CHIPPENDALE DESIGNS

A, These two chairs were made by Benjamin Randolph of Philadelphia *ca.* 1775.
B, The plate is from Chippendale's book first published in 1754.

which the Americans produced by virtue of knowledge, direct or secondhand, of plates in these remarkable books (*Illustration 16*). What was made proved how greatly our cabinetmakers relied on the inspiration provided them by these three English masters of design.

PART TWO

CHAPTER ONE

CHESTS, AND CHESTS OF DRAWERS

THE first settlers brought only those things essential to life in a new, wild land—some live stock, tools, seeds, apparel, bedding, a few books, and the simplest of eating and cooking implements. They did not have to worry as to whether the barrels of dishes would escape breakage if the cargo shifted when the seas ran high, for they lived in an age of wooden trenchers which were service, dinner, and bread-and-butter plates, all in one. Their trunks were simple Tudor chests of various kinds and sizes: large and built of plank for tools; less robust and finer-made for their bedding and whatever clothing was not on the backs of these Puritan and Cavalier colonists. Lastly, there were small, dual-purpose ones which not only stored the treasured seeds, books, and family trinkets but served as writing boxes—the early 17th Century substitute for desks and secretaries.

Their owners were unconscious empire builders, and the humble chests themselves played no mean part in furniture development in the new country. From their original form springs the long line through the blanket to the cedar chest of today without which no bride is decently equipped. Add drawers, and the descendant becomes a chest of drawers. Make it four feet six or taller, and it is a chiffonier. Put it on a frame or trestle, and it starts being a highboy if large, a primitive desk if small. Enclose the elevating supports, make the lid fast, and introduce doors into the upper and lower fronts, and the cupboard is achieved. This last transformation had already been accomplished before America was open to English settlers, but the other variations came about on both sides of the Atlantic afterward. With this generalization of what pieces of furniture were developed from the simple box with lid, we pass to detailed consideration of the chest and its male child, the chest of drawers. The other pieces derived from this common ancestor will be considered later, since an endeavor to include them all in one chapter would produce such confusion that readers could not see the branches of this family tree for the leaves.

Transatlantic shipping, rigor of the early days, and the fires that often destroyed the primitive log and wattle houses wrought such havoc with these imported chests that about the only surviving examples are a few writing or Bible boxes which are found here and there in museums and in the collections of historical societies (*Illustration 17*). Generally of oak and proportioned to hold one of the folio-sized Bibles from the early presses of Geneva or England, they were ornamented, at least on the front, with shallow carving, had a lock of formidable size and the initials of the original owner as part of the decorative carving. They can well be thought of as the bon-voyage gift of the period. The Long Island Historical Society in its collection in Brooklyn, New York, has such a writing box. It was brought from Holland by an ancestress of many of the old Flatbush families, and while of Dutch origin it is in line and execution the same as those known to have come from England.

Not only were these pieces repositories for books, papers, and money and jewelry, if any, but they may perhaps have served as models for the first and plainer chests of larger proportions made in this country. Samples of the latter dating before 1650 are occasionally seen, and save for the fact that they are of wood that grew in the New World, it would be difficult indeed to state positively that they were not made on the eastern shore of the Atlantic. Construction and decorative carving are European, and there are no traces of American individuality. They are memory pieces, and the

Illustration 17. *(Metropolitan Museum of Art)*

A 17TH CENTURY AMERICAN BIBLE BOX

The letters M. H. carved in the front are the initials of the original owner. It is made of oak and ash and dates from the second half of that century.

Illustration 18. *(Gallery of Fine Arts, Yale Univ.)*

A WILLIAM AND MARY BLANKET CHEST

The lid is hinged at the back to give access to the well behind the upper two drawer-fronts that are false. Made in New England between 1690 and 1710.

shallow carving that ornaments the front panels, stiles, and rails is Old World in style and motif.

Even as early as this, some of them have one or two drawers beneath the large compartment—the first step in the evolution of the chest of drawers. At the same time, with ornamental carving omitted and other woods substituted for oak, these early forms with or without drawers continued to be made for more than a hundred and fifty years as blanket chests (*Illustration 18*). Usually of soft wood, they were directly related to the chests of the first half of the 17th Century, although in construction and design they took on refinements of the various style periods in vogue. I have in my collection a typical pine blanket chest made about 1810. Carving of the front has been replaced by false drawers, beneath which is one practical drawer; but the plain top, pin hinges, and simple sides that extend downward to provide legs are in essence, though diluted by two centuries, the specifications of that earlier date.

After 1650, chest making in America struck out for itself. Original Early American furniture began to be produced, and the Connecticut Valley, the new West of the day, was the scene of this most interesting development. Here worked Nicholas Disbrowe, whose inscribed chest, mentioned in Part One, earns for him both respect for his craftsmanship and the title of the first known American cabinetmaker with an example of his work extant. The front of this unique piece is completely covered with an all-over design, not purely English, although Disbrowe had reached his majority before he came to New England. While a conventionalized tulip is the basic motif, there are also suggestions of a similar use of the sunflower which is the dominant motif in most of the Connecticut chests. It also has two drawers where most of the others had one or none. Where he used carved oak, others sometimes achieved decorations with split balusters and oval bosses affixed to the stiles and rails that framed the carved panels. Such chests were originally painted, the background

A

Illustration 19. *(Gallery of Fine Arts, Yale Univ.)*

B

17TH CENTURY CONNECTICUT VALLEY CHESTS

A, Good example of the Connecticut chest with tulip and sunflower decorations. Made 1675 to 1690 in or near Hartford. B, The standard form of the Hadley chest. These are known to have been made as late as about 1720.

of the carving sometimes being done in a dull red with the rest finished in black (*Illustration 19A*). Some were more elaborately colored, yellow flowers, green leaves, and a red or black background while any applied ornaments and molding were finished in yellow or green. Such a piece must have afforded the home of its owner a cheering, colorful note that combined well with bed and wall hangings of crewel embroidery in common use.

At Hadley, Massachusetts, there was another group, probably headed by Captain John Allis, grandnephew of Disbrowe, which produced pieces somewhat different in detail. The sunflower motif and applied balusters and bosses were not used, and the carving was usually an all-over design (*Illustration 19B*). Chest making undoubtedly flourished in other parts of New England and possibly as far south as Virginia. It persisted until the beginning of the 18th Century. Some of them, like the one which had descended in the Choate family of Ipswich, Massachusetts, had turned front feet of William and Mary feeling and moldings applied in geometric pattern (*Illustration 20*).

Nearly a century later the Palatinate Germans of Pennsylvania, commonly known as Pennsylvania Dutch, made an important furniture contribution with their painted chests. Here the structure was of the simplest dovetailed, solid-board type with bracket feet. Beauty was attained by elaborate painted designs done in many colors (*Illustration 21*). What this group knew about color in the home is still not half recognized, although what they made has interested collectors for years. Their polychrome work might well be studied by designers, and could be the inspiration for decorative treatments that would have refreshing sincerity. A breakfast room with its furniture modeled and decorated in the Pennsylvania Dutch manner, for instance, would be a delight.

About the time the Connecticut chests were in their heyday and were becoming imposing pieces of furniture with four drawers arranged in double tiers, the chest of drawers, a case with the top made fast and drawers inserted in the front from top to bottom, made its début. The earliest examples were executed in the same detail as the chest, and the front ornamented with carving of conventionalized design. Generally

Illustration 20. *(Gallery of Fine Arts, Yale Univ.)*

17TH CENTURY OAK CHEST OF DRAWERS

Decorated with moldings in geometric patterns, some of this type bore very elaborate designs in diamond and octagon shapes. Probably made in New England between 1690 and 1700.

they were of oak, and the panel, stile, and rail method of construction followed. Such pieces began to be made about 1675. These and the Connecticut chests themselves are of course rare pieces today and command high prices, but they are still

Illustration 21. *(Pennsylvania Museum, Philadelphia)*

A PENNSYLVANIA GERMAN PAINTED CHEST

Its design done in bright colors combined flowers and animals. It is dated 1796.

found, unrecognized and therefore undervalued, by persevering collectors in out-of-the-way spots.

With the new ideas of the William and Mary period, cabinet-making received an impetus both forceful and revolutionary. There was a sharp break with the old, and chests of drawers began to be made on new lines structurally and ornamentally. The panel, stile, and rail plan disappeared, and the body was made of wide boards dovetailed at the corners. The drawer openings were outlined by single or double half-round moldings planed out rather than attached with nails and glue. The feet were now feet indeed, with bulbous turnings made fast by driving the small end into holes bored at the four corners of the body. Ball and turnip shapes were a characteristic of the period (*Drawing 3*). Along the upper and lower edges of the body a simple molding mitred at the corners gave a needed finish. Use of brass mounts began at this time. They consisted of simple escutcheons for keyholes and unpretentious drops for handles. Instead of ornamenting by carving, cabinet-makers began to make the most of the beauty of grain found in the native hard and soft woods.

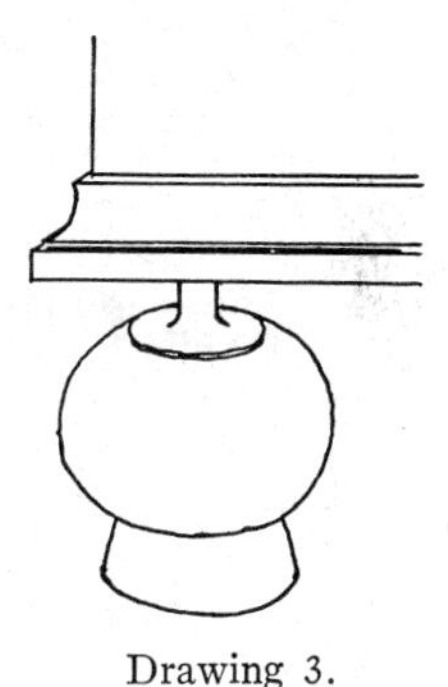

Drawing 3.
A William and Mary bulbous foot.

South of New York, walnut was a favorite, while pine and maple led in popularity in New England. I have studied a tall chest of drawers of this period now owned by Dr. George P. Coopernail of Bedford, New York. It originated in the Housatonic Valley of Connecticut (*Illustration 22*). The drawer fronts are maple which has some curl to its grain. When the present owner first saw this piece, the feet had been replaced by primitive brackets, and its possessor insisted it had "always been that way." During a visit to the attic to look at something else, a box down under the eaves, neglected and forgotten for a hundred years, was pulled out. In it were odds and ends of hardware and—the missing feet! They had probably been re-

Illustration 22. *(Dr. George P. Coopernail)*

A WILLIAM AND MARY TALL CHEST OF DRAWERS

This is an early example of the use of curly maple for drawer-fronts. Made in the Housatonic valley of Connecticut between 1690 and 1720.

moved not long after 1800. Another example of the ageless desire to bring things up to date mingled with the New England aversion to throwing anything away. The latter trait often enables one to undo the various crimes of mutilation, so keep an eye on the attic when hunting antiques on their native heath.

The years of the William and Mary period were comparatively few, and the production of pieces correspondingly small. During this period, however, the chest of drawers became established as a piece of furniture, and its construction took on characteristics that continued until paneled ends, stiles, and rails returned with some of the pieces made in the later Sheraton years.

Drawing 4.
A Queen Anne cabriole leg with pad foot.

Transition to the Queen Anne period was at first chiefly a matter of replacing the bulbous turned feet with a framework base having short turned legs tapering to button-like feet. In the earliest forms, the front and side rails of this frame are plain. Later types transform them into a skirt cut by scroll saw in pleasing valance outlines and combined with a short cabriole leg terminating in a pad foot (*Drawing 4*). Such pieces were made in varying sizes. Some had three tiers of drawers; others had as many as six, increasing in depth as they descended (*Illustration 23*). The cornice moldings were more intricate than those of the William and Mary years, and the finish for the front was achieved by constructing the drawer fronts with a quarter-round lap which concealed the space between drawer and opening. The simple chest with or without one or two drawers was also made with a frame base. These and the chests of drawers on like support are not as common as desks of the same construction, and when located are distinctly worth acquiring. With their articulated and well-modeled legs, cabriole in bend and terminating in a pad sometimes called Dutch foot, these pieces laid the foundation for

Illustration 23. *(Mrs. Homer Eaton Keyes)*

A QUEEN ANNE TALL CHEST OF DRAWERS

The short cabriole legs and base molding are very close to the separate frame sometimes used in that period. This piece is typical of New England work. *Ca.* 1735–1760.

the carved leg with claw-and-ball foot of the Chippendale period.

The bracket foot also came into use during the Queen Anne years. At first it was just what its name suggests, a simple foot made of board, mitred at the corner and scroll-saw cut along the lines of a shelf bracket at the inner side (*Drawing 5*). It was very popular and continued long after this period. Sometimes, to give it further refinement, its perpendicular planes were given a simple cyma curve, and the whole bracket something of the bend of the cabriole, which also

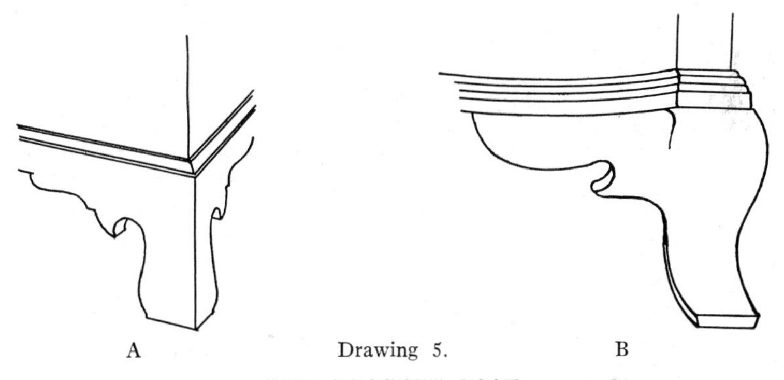

Drawing 5.

THE BRACKET FOOT

A, plain;B, molded and curved.

continued in use for some years. In very carefully designed chests of drawers at this time, added ornamentation was achieved by chamfering the front corners and decorating them with reeding so they resembled pilasters. Also the top projected over the body. Chests-on-chests now appeared and reflected the popularity of the highboy (*Illustration 24*). Most of them have eight or nine tiers of drawers, but occasional examples are found that are a cross between the chest of drawers and the cupboard. The lower section is given over to drawers, while in the upper a pair of paneled doors replace the drawer fronts. Their scarcity and practicality for every-day use make pieces of this sort doubly attractive.

Following the Queen Anne came the so-called early Georgian years when the style known as Chippendale crystallized. As

Illustration 24 A. *(Dr. George P. Coopernail)*

CHEST ON CHEST

A, This is an interesting survival piece. Although predominately Queen Anne in feeling and design it is known to have been made at Cross River, New York, in 1820 as a proof-of-skill piece whereby an apprentice qualified for journeyman standing.

Illustration 24 B. *(American Art Assn.-Anderson Galleries)*

CHEST ON CHEST

B, Chippendale, probably made in Connecticut River valley about 1770.

stated earlier, mahogany came into vogue in this period. Although known since the days of Sir Walter Raleigh and used occasionally by Continental cabinetmakers, this tropical lumber did not gain acceptance here until 1725. But once our craftsmen began to use it, Americans took to it with characteristic enthusiasm and only relinquished it when the black walnut blight put an end to the craft itself. Much of the best furniture of the Chippendale and succeeding periods was made of it, either entirely or in combination with light-colored woods used as inlays or veneers for effective contrast. It was indeed a gratifying wood for cabinetmakers, as it took a high degree of polish, had an attractive grain, and was ideal for carving. This last led to the addition of carved ornamentation, a distinct characteristic of the Chippendale period.

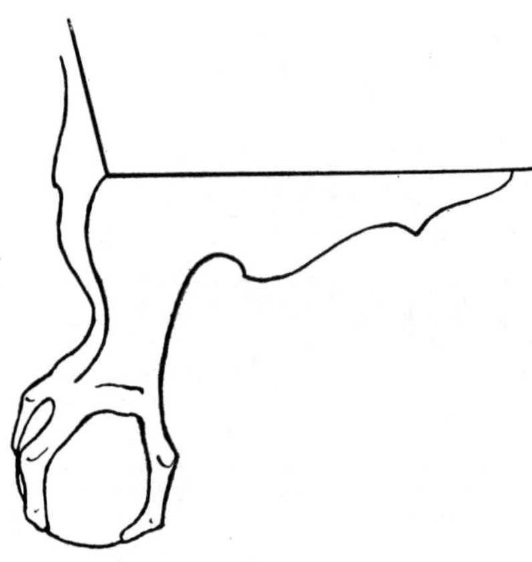

Drawing 6.

A CHIPPENDALE CABRIOLE BRACKET WITH CLAW-AND-BALL FOOT

The bracket foot of the Queen Anne years continued, but the cabriole leg grew a new foot, claw-and-ball in shape (*Drawing 6*). The chests of drawers themselves became more ample of proportion to suit the corresponding size of houses then being built. Put a William and Mary type beside one of the Chippendale era. While there will be little difference in height, the length and breadth of the latter will be just enough greater to give it an impressive Johnsonian air that is a key to all American Chippendale. It was in tune with an age of heavy silks, powdered wigs, and fine broadcloth; an age of formality where the most innocent philanderings were conducted in a ponderous and stilted manner.

In the same way the various style forms mirrored the temper

of different sections of the country. In New England the block-front, in which drawer faces and frame were executed in three vertical panels, the centre one recessed slightly, was the outstanding development. The Townsend-Goddard group led in this and made many beautiful examples (*Illustration 25*). The Philadelphia school of cabinetmakers developed and were

Illustration 25. *(Museum of Fine Arts, Boston)*

A BLOCK–FRONT CHEST OF DRAWERS

It was made by John Townsend of Newport, Rhode Island, in 1792, somewhat later than is generally ascribed to pieces of this design. This indicates how styles persisted after the vogue was supposed to have passed.

partial to the serpentine front. Here, as its name implies, the straight front was supplanted by a delicate curve repeating itself from side to side. Sometimes this serpentine curve was executed with the drawer fronts only, and the top one was given perpendicular rounding so that at the upper edge it conformed with the straight line of the top while the bottom

Illustration 26. *(Gallery of Fine Arts, Yale Univ.)*

A SERPENTINE–FRONT CHEST OF DRAWERS WITH MIRROR TO MATCH

Made by Gostelowe of mahogany throughout save for mirror frame that is gilded pine and probably imported. On a cushion in one of the small drawers, pins form the initials of Gostelowe and his bride. It bears the date 1789 and was made in Philadelphia.

edge was curved to match the outline of those below. In the Pennsylvania Museum in Philadelphia there is a labeled chest of drawers by Jonathan Gostelowe that can well be considered standard for the type made by his contemporaries in this area (*Illustration 26*). Then there was the swell- or bow-front style, a simple arclike curve from side to side, used by cabinet-makers north and south of New York. The latter settlement was still New Amsterdam at heart, and inclined to continue with the somewhat obese Holland designs.

Carved ornamentation was not limited to the claw-and-ball feet and the shaping of the well-sprung cabriole legs. In the New England block-front type, the outer blocks were surmounted with rayed or fluted shells carved in relief while that of the centre depressed section had the shell done in reverse. For this and some of the serpentine fronted pieces, bracket feet were used with the outer sides cut away in molding forms instead of being left flat, which was the more usual treatment for this type of foot. For a finish on the outer edges of the drawers a simple cockle molding was invariably used. Some pieces were further ornamented by a small shell carving placed pendent at the centre of the bottom cross-member. Again, the front corners of certain chests were chamfered and reeded, or quarter-round pilasters similarly treated were used. There are also a few examples with fretwork akin to the best of the Chinese Chippendale. The moldings used at both bottom and top of the body were fashioned by combinations of the cyma curve and were more elaborate than those earlier.

To say that all American Chippendale of first merit was done in mahogany is too sweeping, since some of the best examples in museum collections are of walnut. Such pieces preëminently originated in Pennsylvania or farther South. There are others of cherry, and I once saw an unusually nice chest of drawers made of white wood painted red. These are exceptions, however, and mahogany was the more usual wood. In fact where curly maple is the material, such a piece may be considered transitional and reflecting the oncoming vogue in the

Hepplewhite and Sheraton periods for fancy grained woods. The end of the Chippendale coincides with American history very neatly. The following jingle has long served me as a means of remembering when this style-period ceased to be the dominating factor in our cabinetmaking:

> *American Revolution fought and won,*
> *The style of Chippendale is done.*

To be exact, 1780 marks the turn from elaborate detail to that of the chaste Hepplewhite, which in turn was inspired by the design of the brothers Adam, the Scotch architects who educated the English-speaking world in the restful and compelling beauty of classic simplicity. Perhaps Americans had had enough of royal governors with their magnificent dress and manner of living and were glad to turn from the furniture forms that connoted them. Anyway, turn they did, and rapidly. In a surprisingly short time our cabinetmakers had mastered the new style and were making chests of drawers no less beautiful but different.

Where the Chippendale had dignity of proportions, not unlike that of a well set-up man who is big in every way so that he tips the scales at two hundred pounds or better, the Hepplewhite slogan was "More grace and less bulk." Warmth and color were achieved by the use of inlayed molding and medallions (*Illustrations 27*). Sometimes large flat surfaces done in mahogany were relieved by a mahogany veneer of fine grain that reflected the light. A refinement of this was to place an elliptical panel of very fine crotch-grained veneer in the centre, outline it with a line of white inlay and then cover the rest of the area with veneering of less pronounced grain. This served to frame the central oval and enhance the decorative effect. Any craftsman who did this successfully had an eye for line and simple beauty of no mean order.

The Hepplewhite chests of drawers varied little in shape from those of the Chippendale, though many of them were a little taller, which made it possible to have five instead of four drawers. The serpentine and bow fronts continued. It is below the lower drawer that Hepplewhite influence is most noticeable. No more claw-and-ball feet! The apron connecting the upright supports with a nice serpentine curve makes its appearance, and

Illustration 27. *(Gallery of Fine Arts, Yale Univ.)*

A HEPPLEWHITE BOW-FRONT CHEST OF DRAWERS

Snakewood veneer and lines of inlay are typical of the fancy-grained woods and contrasting inlay then used. More often chests in this style have but four drawers. Dates from *ca.* 1785–1795.

the feet themselves are a distinct modification of the old bracket foot. They are taller and more slender, with an outward splay that is the unmistakable imprint of the period (*Drawing 7*). The use of mahogany still continued, though not by itself. Inlays and fancy grained woods were combined with it.

I once saw a New England chest of drawers which attained unusual beauty by its very simplicity. The body and base were of mahogany with a little inlay of holly. The drawer fronts were all of bird's-eye maple. Into these were set key plates of the red wood of the frame and pulls of the same material. Classically simple in line and proportion, it was both dignified and restful to the eye. Added to this was the contrast of the reddish mahogany frame that served as a background for the light panels of the drawer fronts. The use of mahogany again for the keyhole escutcheons and drawer handles instead of brasses was a stroke of sheer genius. I do not know where this piece is now, but if ever I find it again, it shall be mine though I go hungry and homeless in consequence.

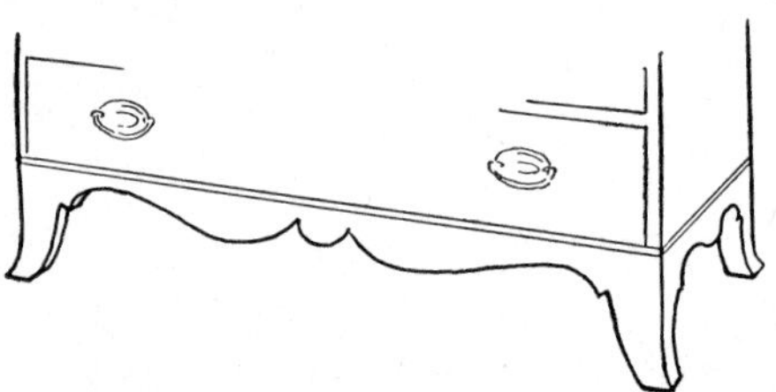

Drawing 7.

A HEPPLEWHITE SPLAYED FOOT WITH VALANCED APRON

On the heels of the Hepplewhite style came that originated by Sheraton, who combined furniture designing with preaching. In general outline the chests of drawers executed under his influence bear a close similarity to the preceding mode (*Illustration 28*). If anything, they are of ampler proportions, and the serpentine front is not employed. Straight and bow fronts were common to both styles, and in Sheraton designs will be found the splayed bracket foot which first came into use with Hepplewhite. The chief characteristics of the Sheraton mode are the reeded leg and column all but disengaged at the front corners of the chest of drawers, and a shaped apron beneath

Drawing 8.

A Sheraton turned and reeded leg.

the lower drawer with more involved curves (*Drawing 8*). There was less use of large areas of light-toned woods and more all-mahogany pieces were common. It was at this time that the cast-glass drawer knobs either of clear, milky, or bluish hue attached by a long bolt, became popular.

Illustration 28. *(Gallery of Fine Arts, Yale Univ.)*

A SHERATON BOW-FRONT CHEST OF DRAWERS

The turned legs and reeded columns are characteristic of the style in America. The grain of the mahogany crotch veneer drawer front is framed for contrast by a border of light-colored wood. *Ca.* 1795–1810.

During the years from the Queen Anne through the Sheraton, the chest-on-chest, or double, continued to be made. It was always of the straight front type, and usually the upper section was a little narrower than the lower. Its various refinements in execution were in accord with the style that ruled at the time it was made.

Shortly after the close of the War of 1812 our American Empire years began. And now the chests of drawers were made on lines that combined the Sheraton with style elements from the French Empire that blossomed when Bonaparte was Napoleon I, Emperor of France, and temporary world-shaker. Here the style elements were carved paw feet (*Drawing 9*) at the front, and columns or pilasters connecting the over-hung top drawer—which might be as deep as or deeper than any of the others—with the feet (*Illustration 29*). A distinct innovation was the use of an upright board at the back of the top from six to twelve inches wide with the upper edge shaped and volute scrolls at the corners. It was a step towards the bureau with mirror as an integral part.

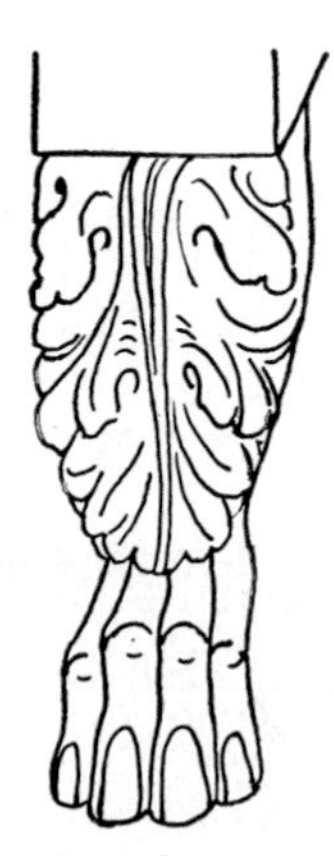

Drawing 9.

American Empire claw foot with leaf carving above.

While a few of the chests of drawers and bureaus had some lightness and grace and were made of contrasting woods, many more were entirely of mahogany with crotch-grain veneering liberally used and were overheavy of line and proportion. Those pieces in which the rounded-edged cockle-molding has given way to the three-tier French are distinctly of the end of this period. In rural areas, the carved paw feet were often replaced by turned ones that inclined to the ponderous. Taste in drawer fronts began to slip, along with other details. When veneered, they were somewhat rounded vertically, and in decadent examples the ogee molding style was rampant.

Typical chests of drawers during the American Empire period were from ten to fourteen inches taller than their predecessors, and some of them had a compartment of shallow drawers attached above the top itself which were about half the depth of the main ones. Wooden knobs or lion's-head brasses with pendent rings were the usual fittings for the drawers. Although many pieces verged on the ungainly for size and proportions, these years saw much of the best mahogany veneering. In some cases the crotch veneer was of such fine grain, the pattern of its application so well balanced, that the piece in total effect rises above its lack of grace.

Illustration 29. (*Mrs. Louis Lee Nichols*)

AN AMERICAN EMPIRE CHEST OF DRAWERS

The paw feet, columns, and crotch mahogany veneer are typical of the style and period. From central New York and made possibly as late as 1835.

Then came the deluge of funereal walnut pieces which, because of lack of grace and craftsmanship, are barred as antiques. They date from 1840 and are the first fruits of the factory production which, nearly a century later, is now beginning to bring forth pieces of inherent merit and good workmanship.

CHAPTER TWO

TABLES, LARGE AND SMALL

An American dinner of the 17th Century. Whether the locale was Virginia, where indentured servants or negroes bore the brunt of toil, or Plymouth with its ceaselessly industrious women-folk, the picture is of an impressively large table groaning under platters of wild and domestic meats, big pitchers of cider and small beer, baked pumpkins, boiled root crops, and a pudding, Indian probably. At one end sits father, a little lordly as befits the master of the house; on either side guests, relatives, children, the latter most emphatically "seen but not heard"; at the other end, mother, hospitably anxious about the quality of the dinner. There is only one thing wrong. Seventeenth Century Americans did not dine thus.

With very rare exceptions their tables were small—hardly large enough for even a modern family. The key to how they ate is probably to be found in the southern mountains. Here 16th and 17th Century domestic customs still rule, and at mealtimes a first and second table is the accepted thing. The men dine first in splendid masculine isolation, then the women and children. Barbaric? Not at all. Just a Tudor custom surviving in a highland backwater. So did the Pilgrims of Plymouth and the first Virginians of the lower James. No woman of those days who respected herself would have done other than wait for the second sitting. What we consider proper-sized dining tables did not come into general use in America until the close of the 18th Century—nor in England for that matter. Study Hogarth's anecdotal drawings, such as "Marriage à la Mode." There are no dining tables, only tea tables for two or four. At a Lord Mayor's banquet or like function the tables are simply long, narrow tops resting on trestles or horses.

Having firmly settled the 17th Century world at small tables, I must admit that in the Metropolitan Museum in New York there is one of refectory proportions which from material and workmanship is properly held to be the oldest American-made table extant (*Illustration 30*). It is twelve feet long by two wide, has a top of one-piece pumpkin pine and three trestle supports of oak. Leonardo da Vinci could have used

Illustration 30. (*Metropolitan Museum of Art*)

AN UNUSUAL 17TH CENTURY AMERICAN TRESTLE TABLE

Top is a pine plank and the underbody oak. *Ca.* 1650. Most tables of this period were small.

it in posing his "Last Supper," for in line and structure it goes back a long way in furniture history. A search for others like it would unearth possibly fifty in all the museums and private collections of the country—obviously the exceptions that prove the small-table rule.

In the construction of the early table, the southern mountaineers again furnish a clue. They still make theirs with a thick board top and three or four rough eight-sided legs that flare outward boldly. Thirty years ago similar types could be seen on Vermont farms in woodsheds, milk rooms, and outbuildings. Made in the early days of pioneering, they are memory pieces, and in design hark back to a type of construction which the first colonists along the Atlantic sea-

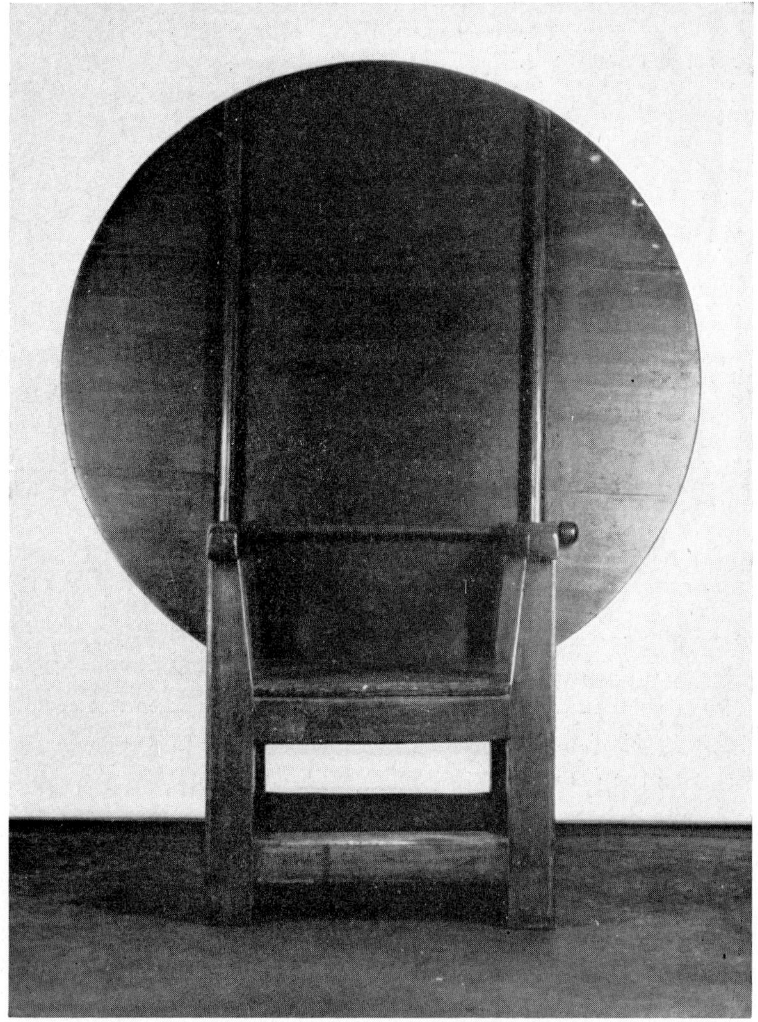

Illustration 31. *(Gallery of Fine Arts, Yale Univ.)*

PURITAN CENTURY TABLE-CHAIR

Its base is similar to that of the wainscot chairs of the period. Because of the heaviness of its base this piece would seem to antedate 1675.

board brought with them from across the water. In cant of leg there is a Windsor chair flavor which both pieces of furniture undoubtedly derived from the crude peasant style of the Gothic years.

Aside from the Metropolitan's remarkable refectory table, other surviving examples of the first half of the 17th Century are, the gate-leg with round or oblong top of small, medium, or, occasionally, large size; the trestle-based ones with tops of the same sort, and the dual-purpose pieces. These last include the various forms of the hutch table-chair—that ingenious piece which, with the top swung vertical, became an armchair—and the combination of table and chest, where a shallow chest resting on turned legs is of such height that with lid flat it can perform its table function as adequately as if there were no storage space beneath. The combination of chair and table is of course a furniture form that is still made. Go to the unpainted furniture section of almost any department store, and you will find it offered not as a reproduction but simply as a practical piece of furniture made primarily in the double chair size. Some of these modern adaptations even include a chest feature concealed beneath the hinged seat (*Illustration 31*).

The first colonists had need of these dual-purpose pieces as well as tables with very narrow bed and wide leaves called "tuck-aways," for their houses were small, and what living-room space there was had to serve for all uses. In inventories around the year 1650, this space that was living room, dining room, kitchen, and workshop is referred to as "hall," a designation dating from the simple manor houses of England, where one room so called was exactly that. In describing the furnishings of these American halls, appraisals show that several tables valued at small sums were the standard equipment. Occasionally a "turned table" of substantially greater value is included. The gate-leg, for instance, was no rudely made piece, but an excellent example of the best table thoughts of both England and America (*Illustration 32*).

In Governor Edward Winslow's Plymouth home there was one, now shown in Pilgrim Hall, that must have ranked as very large. Whether such tables had, like the Winslow one, a span of approximately four feet or were much smaller, the construction was the same. The supporting framework was in design very close to that of the joined stools then in use but of larger proportions. The legs were vase-shaped turnings, and connecting them was a double set of stretchers either square

Illustration 32. *(Gallery of Fine Arts, Yale Univ.)*

A PENNSYLVANIA GATE–LEG TABLE

Larger tables of this design had double supporting legs on each side. Made between 1725 and 1750. The wood is walnut.

or turned, one set immediately beneath the top and the other a few inches from the floor. To support the leaves when raised there were either two or four supplemental legs. These and the stretchers connecting them to the rigid frame were so near in outline to that of a garden gate that the name readily attached itself (*Drawing 10*). Tops were square, oblong, round, or oval as taste and use dictated. Some of the frames were elaborate in execution, others were simple. They were made of all sorts of native woods, but the under structure was usually of hard wood even if the top was pine. Fine examples made all of walnut, maple, cherry, or the like were produced both North and South through the 17th and well into the 18th Century. Unfortunately the joiners in various parts of

Drawing 10.

GATE-LEG TABLE CONSTRUCTION

Supporting leg swung beneath raised leaf.

the country did not employ differences of turning marked enough to enable one to judge whether a table originated in Massachusetts or Pennsylvania. As a general rule, however, those of walnut were made south of New York, while those of maple or cherry are of New England origin.

I once saw one of this type in which the turned body was of pear wood and the top of apple that had been made at Hampton, New Hampshire, very early. The hardness of the pear wood—it is the finest grained of all our native fruit woods and chiefly used for tool handles—had preserved the details of the turnings and the outline of the button feet almost as they came from the lathe. This is unusual. In most gate-leg tables the feet either have worn away or have broken

Illustration 33. *(Gallery of Fine Arts, Yale Univ.)*

A SMALL TAVERN TABLE

The turning of legs, feet, and knobs are finer and better preserved than are usually found. This was made of walnut early in the 18th Century.

and therefore been cut off, and the turnings of the cross-members are flattened on the upper side by the generations of feet that have rested on them.

All through the William and Mary and Queen Anne periods

the gate-leg table held its public, as it were, but neither of these styles seems to have had any modifying influence on the details of the turnings, which by individual whim varied from a vase-shape with unbroken lines to ring-and-ball turnings alternated in profusion. Some of these tables were made of mahogany, which puts them as late as the second quarter of the 18th Century. But though they submitted to the changing style in wood, their design and execution remained essentially 17th Century.

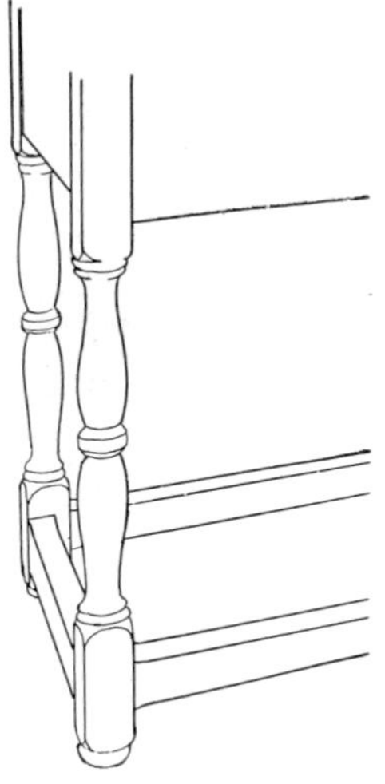

Drawing 11.

The turned uprights and plain stretchers of a tavern table.

Contemporary with the gate-leg is the tavern table, which was executed in a number of forms. The earliest seem to have been those with a simple frame and a board top (*Illustration 33*). This frame was made with four corner posts or legs turned in an elongated vase-shape between the upper and lower square sections, where, with tenons, mortises, and pins, plain stretchers were attached. The lower of these, about two inches above the floor, were made from squared material about an inch and a half by two inches and a half. The upper stretchers, with their upper edge flush with the tops of the posts, were of the same thickness but might be as much as four inches wide. Below the lower stretchers the legs terminated in simple feet, button- or pear-shaped (*Drawing 11*). While all this was usually made of hard-wood, the top was often one or two pieces of pine finished with end-strips to hold them together and prevent warping. As time went on, the dimensions of this type increased; the upper stretchers took on apron proportions, and one or two drawers were added. Tavern tables of this sort, made in Pennsylvania or farther south of walnut, are fairly common, and some have tops up to four feet long by three wide. They make excellent library tables and so bring good if not high prices. Occasionally one is found that is five feet long and was probably the *table d'hôte* of a tavern. It is ideal for a dining table in a country home.

While the one in my collection has legs square from top to bottom, its unusual dimensions—length, six feet four inches; breadth, two feet seven; and height, two feet four inches—make it so satisfactory as a dining table that I overlook the lack of turnings of the corner posts. The top is of two pieces of pine with end strips. The frame is a mixture

Illustration 34. *(Author's collection)*

A LARGE BUT LATE TAVERN TABLE

The square legs show this is a rural survival piece. It was found near Warrensburg, New York. It may have been made by some rural craftsman as late as 1820.

of maple, birch, and beech. I do not delude myself. It is a 19th Century, farm-made survival, but what should be expected for fifteen dollars (*Illustration 34*)? It came from upper New York State. I saw it before an antique shop while passing on a bus. True to form, I alighted and walked back, looked the table over, casually I thought, and then entered. I looked at several things, asked prices, and then off-handedly priced my table. A little further prowling and another casual inquiry about the table. No difference in price, and as it was really a bargain, I paid for it.

"I saw you eye that table from the bus and again when you came in and knew if I sold you anything it would be that piece," the dealer commented dryly as he folded away my money and shipping address. "I can tell what a person really wants before they've been in my shop five minutes, and tell the lookers too. If there is something a customer wants, you can tell it by their eye. They are worth bothering with.

Illustration 35. *(American Art Assn.—Anderson Galleries)*

A CURLY MAPLE BUTTERFLY TABLE

Such tables developed along with the tavern type and were made very late in the 17th and early in the 18th Century.

But lookers! I tell 'em anything and don't bother my head about 'em. I'm here to sell; not to run a museum."

Along with the tavern table of rectangular outline there was another in which the legs flared out to the sides after the manner of the first crude tables and some of the joined stools. With the earliest, the flaring leg is the only change. Later came drop-leaves, and two swinging supports shaped like the wing of a butterfly which gave this type of table its name (*Illustration 35*). They, like the smaller sizes of tavern table, are found with rectangular, oval, or round tops and date from about the second or third decade of the 18th Century. They are found infrequently, and because of their real beauty command corresponding prices.

The William and Mary style brought nothing to table design in America, but, during the Queen Anne years, cabinetmakers broke sharply with the old frame construction and brought forth a type in which the bottom stretcher disappeared entirely and the upper ones became the only structural cross pieces. The straight, postlike supports made way for nicely curved cabriole legs that terminated in simple pad feet (*Drawing 12*). With medium-sized tables, leaves, supported by concealed brackets or legs that swung outward, were typical. In those of smaller size and leafless, the cross members were widened to apron proportions, and the lower edge scalloped with the curves so characteristic of the period and explained more fully in the description of the Queen Anne chests of drawers.

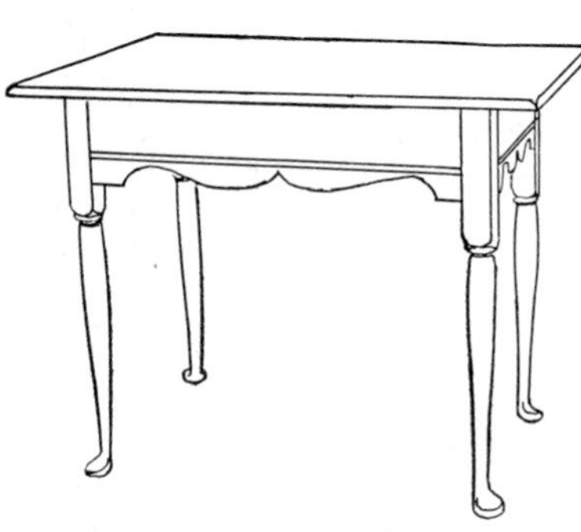

Drawing 12.

AN EARLY QUEEN ANNE TEA TABLE

The simple turned legs and curved apron are characteristic of the start of this period.

It was an age of tea drinking, and possession of a nicely made and delicate table bespoke social standing. So many fine tea tables were fashioned in walnut, plain and fancy grain maple, and mahogany (*Illustration 36*). Along with these there may have been a few pier tables—they were very popular in England—made in America; but they are so rare that for practical purposes they can be disregarded save as their elaborate carving served as the entering wedge for the style of Chippendale. With rare exceptions the carved ornamentation

A

Illustration 36. B (*Gallery of Fine Arts, Yale Univ.*)

TWO QUEEN ANNE TABLES

A, The heavy raised molding around the rectangular top forms a tray, and the bracketed skirt is elaborately scrolled with central pendants. Of Connecticut origin and made between 1730 and 1750. B, Round table with drop leaves and two swinging legs of cabriole line ending in Dutch feet.

of American-made pieces did not take on the over-elaborate characteristics of some of the pieces made in England. When our craftsmen made tables in the Chippendale manner, they held themselves within bounds. The cabriole leg of former years simply had added to it the claw-and-ball foot, and sometimes shell carving ornamented the knee.

The Townsend-Goddard group produced some very fine

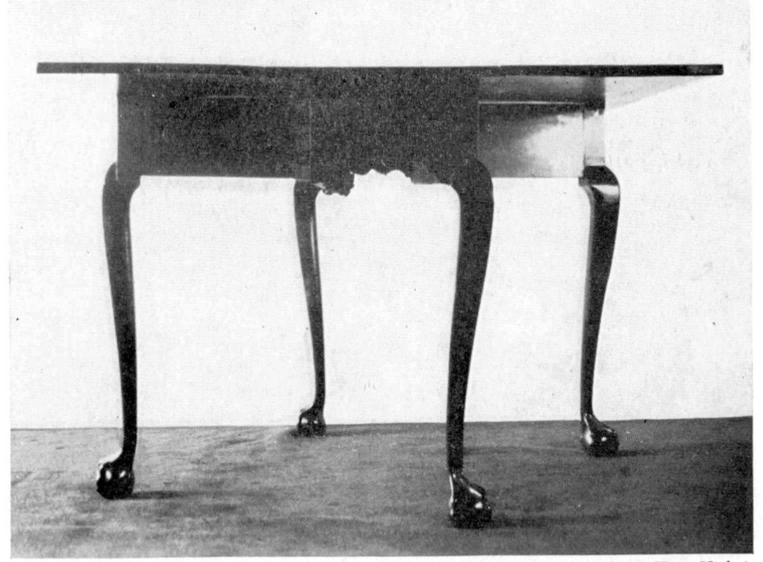

Illustration 37. *(Gallery of Fine Arts, Yale Univ.)*

A CHIPPENDALE TABLE

It has cabriole legs and claw-and-ball feet. Made of mahogany and typical of the larger tables of this period. Massachusetts, 1760–1770.

tea tables with an oblong tray-top shaped by ogival curves after the manner of their block-front secretaries and chests of drawers. The cabriole legs were ornamented with carving at both knee and foot. The apron or frieze conformed to the block shaping of the top, which was without leaves and had its outer edge framed with a raised molding of nicely executed cyma curves. This last not only was ornamental but served as a guard for the fine Lowestoft tea sets just coming into fashion (*Illustration 36*). Made all in mahogany, such a table can well be considered the high point of Chippendale work as far as this piece is concerned.

But the majority of American Chippendale tables were not as elaborate. Also they were larger. Usually the bed was fairly narrow, and two wide leaves supported by brackets or swinging legs gave the top a fair-sized area when raised (*Illustration 37*). In some, the aprons at the ends were scalloped on the lower edge to give a pleasing arch rather than a straight line. There were two distinct vogues in legs: the curved cabriole just described, and the perfectly straight leg of the same size from top to bottom with a slight chamfer on the inner edge. Where in the Hepplewhite years to come this straight leg would taper downward, it was now of the same cross section its entire length. No carving was used, but the outer edges were given a sunken bead or molding, or the outer sides were similarly ornamented by planing that gave the entire width a slight cut-in finish (*Drawing 13*).

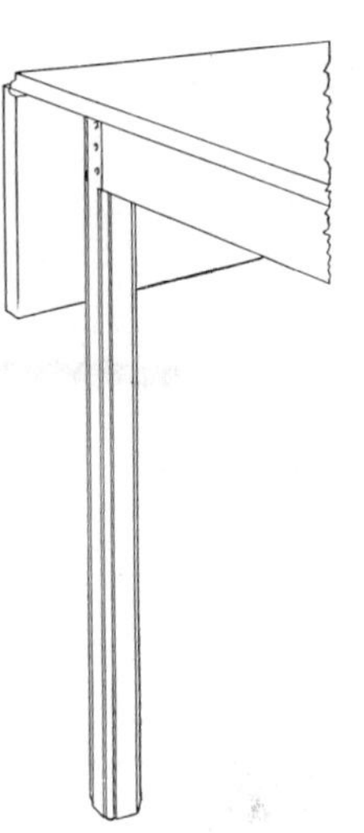

Drawing 13.

A SQUARE CHIPPENDALE LEG

Rule-joint beading cut on outer edge.

A table with these square legs, oblong leaves not too wide, and diagonal stretchers attached to the legs twelve to fifteen inches from the floor to form an X-shaped cross is known as a Pembroke. According to tradition, Thomas Chippendale himself designed this type for the Countess of Pembroke and named it in her honor. A very fine one made by John Townsend and bearing his label was sold at one of the large New York auctions in 1930 (*Illustration 38*). This particular table also had fretwork and other details of the Chinese Chippendale influence which American cabinetmakers generally did not employ.

Like the Queen Anne, this period also produced an innovation in table construction. This was the circular-topped table supported by a central column and three branching feet (*Illustration 39*). Since most of these had the top hinged so that it could be brought into the vertical when not in use, this

Illustration 38. (*American Art Assn.–Anderson Galleries*)

A PEMBROKE TABLE IN THE CHINESE CHIPPENDALE STYLE

The square legs are ornamented with fluting from stretchers to bed. Chinese characteristics decorate the diagonal stretchers and the brackets connecting legs and bed. It bears the label of John Townsend, Newport, Rhode Island, and was made between 1760 and 1770.

style is known as the tilt top. When the circumference of the top was ornamented with a raised molding, it was known as a pie-crust table. Some of these were perfectly round, while with the more elaborate, the edge was scalloped, a detail which enhanced its beauty and made its resemblance to the standard American dessert even more realistic. With these tables the top was attached to the underbody by a pair of cleats running across the underside. Sometimes at the upper end of the

Illustration 39. (*Dr. George P. Coopernail*)

A CHIPPENDALE PIE-CRUST TABLE

Carving ornaments the feet and knees. The central column is turned and fluted. The scalloped raised edge of the top gives this type its name. Found in Hudson River valley; the inference is that it might have been made in New York between 1760 and 1780.

supporting column there was a square boxing, the upper piece of which fitted into these cleats and provided the hinge. It was called a birdcage for its obvious, if remote, resemblance to the latter. The central support was a vase-shaped turned column with three branching legs, of flattened cabriole design with claw-and-ball feet, attached to its base by dovetailing. Tables of this type in original condition usually have a wrought-iron, three-pronged piece which, screwed in place,

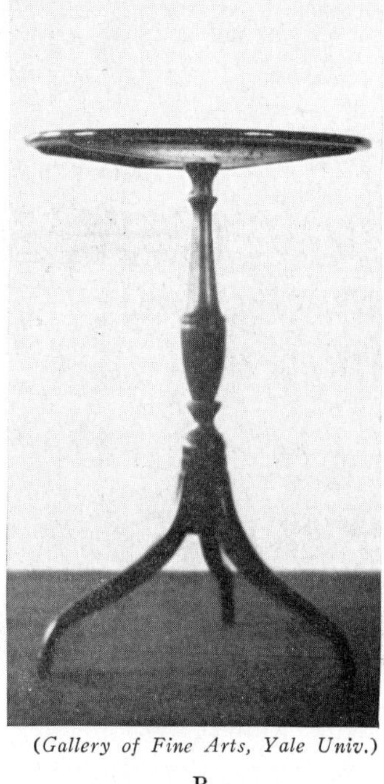

Illustration 40. *(Gallery of Fine Arts, Yale Univ.)*

A B

TWO TRIPOD CANDLE STANDS

A is of Hepplewhite lines; B, of Sheraton. Both are New England pieces. The former was made slightly before 1800, and the latter a few years later.

strengthens this joining of legs and column in a practical and efficient manner.

During the Chippendale years, the tops of such tables were usually not under thirty inches in diameter and were circular. Under the Hepplewhite and Sheraton influence, the design of the legs was simplified from the claw-and-ball foot, and the top was square, oblong, or lozenge-shaped. Many of these later variations were made much smaller to serve as stands for candles or the first of the oil lamps. They were produced

Illustration 41. *(American Art Assn.–Anderson Galleries)*

A CHIPPENDALE CARD TABLE

The shaping of the bed, carving on the knees of the cabriole legs, and execution of the claw-and-ball feet indicate the work of John Goddard of Newport, Rhode Island, about 1760.

from our native hard woods, and an inlay medallion sometimes decorated the centre of the top (*Illustration 40*). From the number that survive, curly maple seems to have been the popular wood. With this there was very little effort made to achieve ornamentation by variation in turning of the central column or by careful articulation of the legs. Rather the variegated grain of the wood itself was relied on as a substitute. Also the top was often made fast to the column in these later types and when found is a sign of early 19th Century production.

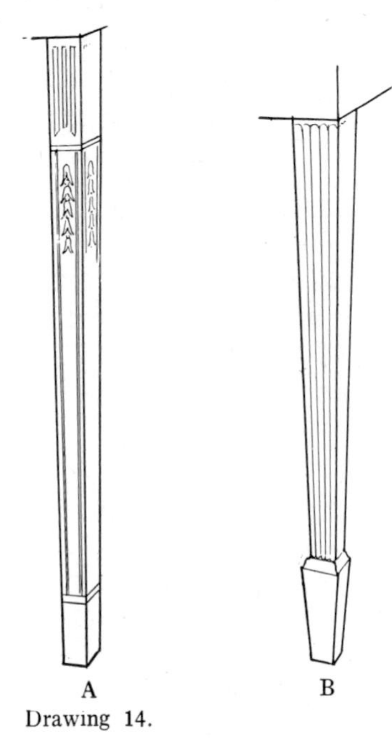

Drawing 14.

HEPPLEWHITE TAPERED LEGS

A, ornamented with inlay; B, fluted and terminating with spade feet.

The card table with double top is also a design that came with the Chippendale period and continued in popular favor through our Empire mode. Here the distinguishing feature is the single leaf of exactly the same size and shape as the fixed top. This, attached with a special type of hinge, can either rest flat on the top or be swung over so that it doubles the area of the top. Again, when the piece stands against the wall, one can raise the leaf to the vertical and have a pier table. Since they were designed chiefly for gaming, some had shallow, bowl-like depressions carved in the top for the coin of the players (*Illustration 41*). Such examples were usually from the shops of craftsmen living south of New York. Evidently the New England conscience would allow card playing, but frowned so effectively on playing for stakes that tables which frankly admitted the latter were not often made within its jurisdiction.

The Hepplewhite style brought in the delightfully simple and graceful tapered leg, which replaced the carved and curved cabriole with its claw-and-ball foot (*Drawing 14*). Straight lines were now the rule. No carving, few curves, right angles principally. For ornamentation, medallion and pencil-line inlays accentuated the simplicity of these pieces. And now came the large dining table (*Illustration 42*). This forerunner of the extension table was produced in two, three, and four parts. With all in use and all leaves raised, a table of three or four sections became a banquet board seating from sixteen to twenty-four people. In essence these sets consisted of two end tables half round in shape, with or without wide oblong leaves attached to the straight edge, and one or two central tables with wide leaves supported by swinging legs. The banquet table at Mount Vernon is of this sort. Probably most well-furnished homes in those days boasted a multiple-unit dining table.

New York's City official banqueting board displayed in the Governor's Room at the City Hall is a table of this sort in *five* parts. With reeded Sheraton legs, end tables that are leafless and have rounded corners, and three centre sections with abnormally wide leaves, when all are raised it is twenty-five feet long. This remarkable mahogany table, undoubtedly part of the original furnishings of the building, was therefore made in 1812, probably under the supervision of John McComb, the architect. Here we have mute evidence of the size of formal dinners where such mayors as Philip Hone and the Common Council entertained corporately New York's distinguished guests before banquets of this sort went out of fashion.

The cabinetmaker who first thought of this essentially practical design accomplished something original that is usable even today. Its flexibility is quite surprising. For a small family the centre section is adequate, and the ends placed against opposite walls become convenient serving tables. By adding sections and raising leaves the table expanse can be gradually increased until at its maximum it is large enough for

Illustration 42. *(Ginsburg & Levy, Inc.)*

A HEPPLEWHITE TWO-PART DINING TABLE

They were also made with one or two central tables for greater length. *Ca.* 1790 a dinner party of imposing proportions. Unfortunately, through the years, these old table sections have become separated. Occasionally one can be found complete. More often sections of identical dimensions and designs have to be gathered one at a

Illustration 43. *(Metropolitan Museum of Art)*

A SHERATON TABLE BY PHYFE

The treatment of the legs is typical of his work. *Ca.* 1810.

time, slowly and patiently. Only occasionally is a complete set found in New England. A much likelier hunting ground is south of New York. In an antique shop in Alexandria, Virginia, I once saw five or six sets of dining tables complete. Inquiry developed that they had all been bought by this dealer within a range of fifty miles. Evidently the three-part table in Hepplewhite, Sheraton, or Empire style was well suited to Virginian hospitality and found ready sale in this market.

The small candle-stand, with top fourteen to twenty inches square, supported by tapered legs was another development of this period; and it, too, continued to be made until the end of our Empire years. During the Sheraton era, a variation of it was the sewing table. Here two shallow drawers were added and beneath them a deep basket covered with silk that moved into place like a drawer. This last acted as storage space for needlework in process of completion. To find a table with its original covering of basket section is almost impossible, for obvious reasons. Replacing it is a simple matter. The old fabrics were laid in pleats running up and down, and the inside was lined with an unfigured material, sometimes silk, but more often linen.

While straight lines and classic simplicity may be the Nirvana of art, the general public prefers it in small doses. So the curves, reedings, and rope turnings of the Sheraton period were grateful sights for eyes grown weary of gazing on the severely chaste examples of the preceding years. In size and slenderness, Sheraton tables followed the example set by Hepplewhite (*Illustration 43*). The legs were turned and in simpler tables ornamented by small ring turnings. In more elaborate forms the plain turned leg was reeded, and occasionally this reeding was varied by a spiral twist known as rope turning. The body and leaves of many of the card tables were shaped with serpentine curves. Here and with some of the smaller light stands, the legs were attached to the body in such a way as to become boldly curved pilasters, and the top was shaped so that the semicircular corners acted as capitals for the column forms of the legs. Inlays were liberally used to ornament Sheraton pieces. Sometimes lines and medallions—a patriotic emblem was popular—and sometimes panels of bird's-eye or curly maple were skillfully employed. In simpler pieces of rural make, the table frame was often of mahogany, cherry, or red walnut, and drawer fronts and tops were of curly or bird's-eye maple.

Duncan Phyfe produced many Sheraton tables that, with their fine proportions and simple beauty, should rank in favor with his more elaborately carved Empire pieces.

"Phyfe tables done in the Sheraton style with reeded legs and shaped leaves are beautiful pieces and representative of

Illustration 44. *(Author's collection)*

A PEDESTAL TABLE OF THE EMPIRE PERIOD

Originally from South Lancaster, Massachusetts, it was probably made in Boston about 1825. The top rotates to give access to the storage space beneath. Nothing but mahogany was used anywhere in this piece, which is unusual for American work.

his best work, but people won't buy 'em," a New York dealer who has handled many examples of this craftsman's work once told me. "No, they want his Empire pieces with pedestal base. They don't think it can be Phyfe unless it has a pedestal. So these fine early pieces go for half the price of those later and sometimes poorer designed ones with a central support."

Occasionally a Sheraton table was produced with the tapered legs so characteristic of Hepplewhite. Here the legs were given a slight outward flare, and the taper was accentuated at the lower ends by delicate spade feet shaped as their name implies.

The last step in antique furniture history, a combination of Sheraton and the French style of Napoleon, developed the table with pedestal base and substituted carving of the acanthus leaf design for reeding. Phyfe's pedestal tables represent the best of this style. Here a severely simple column is supported by four legs that curve concavely toward the floor and terminate in brass claw feet (*Illustration 44*). Sometimes the column is turned in urn shape, and laurel leaf carving ornaments both column and legs. He used this design for centre and three-part dining tables, varying it slightly by the use of three legs instead of four for sewing, pier, and two-part dining tables—a good style, though verging on the ornate, when used by a man of judgment and restraint. Unhappily, more than one cabinetmaker in those last years had neither. Then the turned column became literally covered with acanthus leaves, while under the generous ministrations of the carving tool, the simple curved legs took on a marked resemblance to those of a huge bird of prey and terminated in pronounced talonlike feet.

Toward the close of this period, carving gave way to veneer, and tables with central columns eight to ten inches in diameter and a supporting base with a heavy block or ball foot were the result. Here again misplaced zeal sometimes made the column eight-sided, and with centre tables rested a huge circular or octagonal top on it. Double-topped card tables were also made with pedestal base. With a simple column and well shaped legs they are desirable pieces; but it was a decadent age in furniture history, and one must choose with caution. Among the atrocities should be included those with heavy, cumbersome lyre bases. Here the grace and delicacy of Phyfe's sofa tables of twenty years previous is replaced by a sprawling lyre shape made of veneered wood two inches square and bearing only remote resemblance to the lightsomeness of the New York master's work.

In Empire tables with the usual arrangement of legs—one at each corner and perhaps two swinging ones to support raised leaves—ornamentation by acanthus-leaf carving was frequently effective and of fair artistic merit. But only too soon the legs grew heavy, were made with a little turning at top and bottom and the intervening space square or eight-sided. Such tables are decadent and should be avoided, no matter how excellent the mahogany in them may be. Sometimes marks of later attempts to improve them will be found, the legs, for instance, having been sent back to the lathe and the square or octagon sections reworked into a reeded imitation of Sheraton. It deceives nobody who knows his furniture history. The entire leg is much heavier than the typically reeded one of earlier days, and the ring turnings that form the foot do not follow the former lines.

As stated before, the more ponderous Empire pieces became, the finer the wood. Indeed, the amount of first-grade Santo Domingo mahogany consumed to make this bulky furniture is appalling. But not even beautiful wood could compensate for ungainly outline. The Gilbert and Sullivan quatrain sums up most aptly what happened to American tables as the Empire years progressed.

Stouter than I used to be,
Still more corpulent grow I—
There will be too much of me
In the coming by and by!

CHAPTER THREE

FOUR–POSTERS, HIGH AND LOW

THE earliest American settlers slept close to the floor if not on it. Just what their beds were like cannot be stated with any certainty, as none of them have survived. There is a form used by the mountaineers in the southern Appalachian highlands that doubtless approximates our first type of frame. They call it a jack bed and it consists of a single post set about six feet from one wall and four feet from another. From it, side rails extend to the two walls, and others are attached to them to provide the necessary support for slats or springy poles on which is laid the baglike tick filled with straw, reeds, or fine-cut rags, as the case may be. Beds of such Spartan simplicity existed in England years before the migration to America was thought of, and their survival in the isolated southern mountains is an unconscious remembrance of the ways of the homeland.

But the settlers of the coastal colonies did not adhere to this crude form long. Within twenty-five years after the first Pilgrim clambered out on Plymouth Rock to dry land, bed frames more nearly in accord with the ideas of Tudor England, though not so large or impressive as the "Great Bed of Ware," were in use. They were frames simple in execution but complete. The corner posts were tall enough to support cross pieces from which enclosing curtains could be hung. In the latter lay the decorative emphasis rather than in the woodwork. Some of these first colonists, both North and South, had beds with silken curtains which were quite ostentatious for that day. Commoner materials were of woolen, linen, or patchwork, some thing like the quilts of later date. These were found only in the best rooms of the wealthiest homes. Here also built-in affairs differing little from the slaw beds of Holland were constructed in cubicles opening directly off main rooms. Again,

Illustration 45. (*Metropolitan Museum of Art*)

A LATE 17TH CENTURY FOLDING BED

A lattice of rope supported the mattress. The lower part folded behind curtains hung from the tester at the head.

for economy of space (the 17th Century houses were invariably small), folding beds that could stand in the parlor were popular (*Illustration 45*). Here the frames of simple squared wood had tall posts at the head to which were attached crosspieces for curtains. The side-rails were equipped with ingenious hinged joints about eighteen inches or two feet from the head. By this means the rest of the bed could be raised and concealed behind the curtains. The latter, ornamented with worsted needlework, lent a note of color to the room and were a primitive version of the present-day sleeping equipment that disappears behind doors so popular in contracted city apartments.

Bed hangings had another use besides that of decoration. They were drawn at night like the curtains of a Pullman berth for privacy. With the continued flow of guests and contracted quarters, two double beds in one room were not considered improper. The curtains also provided warmth and shielded the occupants from the drafts characteristic of the houses, which were particularly noticeable at night, when all hearth fires were either banked or extinguished. The phrase "curtain lecture" is thus explained. Retired and somewhat imprisoned by the drawn hangings, many a man had to let his better half express herself freely on his shortcomings. It was take it or climb forth into the cold. I never see one of these beds complete with hangings but I visualize Mr. and Mrs. Pepys. There are a number of entries in his diary regarding such nocturnal broadcasts. Did he eye an actress too closely, or was he surprised parleying with Deborah, their comely serving maid? That night Mrs. Pepys would loose her tongue and might not silence it until the wee hours of morn.

The beds that stood in the main living rooms, turned out with the best hangings the family could afford or its womenfolk produce, have been alluded to already. Here flourished that most peculiar courting custom of Welsh origin known as bundling. Houses were ill heated and winter evenings were bitter in the new land. So this custom of a courting couple, fully dressed—"to prevent scandal," as one chronicler put it—spending the evening in the living-room bed grew up and was prevalent in country areas throughout New England and parts of Pennsylvania until late in the 18th Century. About 1785 a bit of doggerel known as "A New Bundling Song" was printed in an almanac. It was widely read and even appeared as a broadside. Though in even worse taste than the custom itself, its exceedingly broad lines probably did more than anything else to stamp out this questionable practice.

The William and Mary and Queen Anne periods had little effect on beds in this country. It was not until the Chippendale influence reached our shores that frames became other than simple uprights and crosspieces. The day-bed was an exception.

Illustration 46. *(Gallery of Fine Arts, Yale Univ.)*

A WALNUT DAY–BED

The back and seat are cane. In design it is Carolean, and the carved feet are of the Spanish type. Of New England origin, its date is *ca.* 1700–1720.

It reached America with the last years of the Stuart kings and was made in the ornate style of the Restoration. In outline it was a chair with the seat lengthened to six feet, and four or six supplemental legs added. Life in America was already becoming easier, and it is comforting to realize that the colonists, despite their reputation for ceaseless industry, occasionally took an hour out for daytime napping (*Illustration 46*).

While these day-beds were influenced in detail by the various style periods—late Carolean, William and Mary, Queen

Anne, and Chippendale—they more or less followed the same lines structurally. They had eight legs, an elongated seat and a back or headpiece somewhat lower than that of a chair. The headpiece was either built with a backward slope or made movable so that one could set the angle to suit one's taste and comfort. When cane was not used for the back and body, upholstery, generally leather, was employed. In some the

Illustration 47.

A LOW BED OF SHAKER MAKE

Members of this sect made large quantities of furniture, especially chairs, at their various colonies which they sold commercially. This bed, which may have been made as late as 1850, is provided with large wooden casters. In design their furniture reverted to early colonial lines.

back was executed with upright splats which obviated the need of covering there. A very few pieces were made wider than usual and provided with a mattress or pad that made them adequate for a night's sleep in an emergency. The rarity of these early day-beds is shown by the fact that in the largest collections dispersed at auction, not more than two or three will be found at any one sale, though it may include several fine examples of carved Connecticut chests, in themselves rare enough to be museum specimens in practically any degree of ornamentation.

At the same time as these interesting and useful pieces were being made for the affluent colonists, particularly in southern New England and Pennsylvania, the general run of joiners continued to make bed frames of the simplest sort—just posts and rails squarely geometric in outline, and headboard a simple cross member of unornamented board to retain pillows. Those for important rooms had tall posts to support the tester framework; lesser beds were frequently very low and almost fundamental in structure. Four short uprights, those at the foot extending just an inch or so above the upper surface of the rails while those at the head were eight to twelve inches higher so that the ends of the headboard might fit into them. They were just right for the low, sloping-ceiling rooms so often found on the second floor of early one-story houses. So they earned the name of under-eaves beds (*Illustration 47*).

This design was not stopped by the Chippendale influence, but continued in the more isolated country communities until about 1820. The earlier types are of lighter proportions, but some of the later ones had turned rather than square or octagonal legs. These taper slightly, and though innocent of ornamental rings and vase shapings are pleasing in their simplicity and quite usable today in country homes of the simpler sort.

Beds for babies and children of the first two centuries in America were as important as those for adults. The yearly baby was the accepted rule, and so both cradles and small beds were necessary. The wicker cradle of Peregrine White, whose arrival took place aboard the *Mayflower* as it lay at anchor in Massachusetts Bay, and whose death was so long delayed that our first tabloid, the Boston *News Letter,* carried his obituary in its fourth issue, was not a model for those of contemporary children. The first cradles made here were panel-sided affairs much like the chests of the period with lid omitted and rockers added. Later editions were embellished with a wooden hood or canopy at the upper end. Then came cradles with sides that flared upward and outward. These, made with or without a hood and a framework mortised or dovetailed at the corners, remained the order of the day well into the 19th Century.

Stephen A. Douglas, known as the Little Giant, Lincoln's outstanding political opponent, made such a cradle during the time he was apprenticed to Nahum Parker, the cabinetmaker of Middlebury, Vermont, where it is still preserved by the Williamson family for whom it was made. To this day, each new baby is ceremoniously rocked once in it and then transferred with all speed to a more scientific though less artistic contraption with wire sides and rockerless legs. This is about as good a use as can be found for these old pieces, for in all honesty, like the spinning wheel, they are interesting but out-of-date. I do know of a writer who uses one as a filing case for his manuscripts. As a resting place for his brain children it serves excellently until some one unwittingly steps on one of the long rockers and catapults the contents to the floor. Then, during the long hours of sorting, this new use does not seem so happy.

As soon as the child was a year old, he graduated from the cradle to a trundle or truckle bed. This, fashioned on the same lines as the under-eaves bed only lower and smaller, was a piece of furniture descended from the Middle Ages. In those days an important warrior, to insure being alive in the morning, had his most trusted retainer sleep at his feet in a bed that was the original of the trundle but of full size. Whether the earliest American trundle beds were intended to be concealed beneath the larger one during daylight hours is not clear. Certainly it was the custom in later years, when three-inch wooden wheels were set into the legs to facilitate rolling. Being strictly utilitarian pieces, they seem not to have been affected by stylistic changes. From the earliest examples down to the days of Andrew Jackson they varied practically not at all in outline or construction, and they were made of all kinds and mixtures of wood.

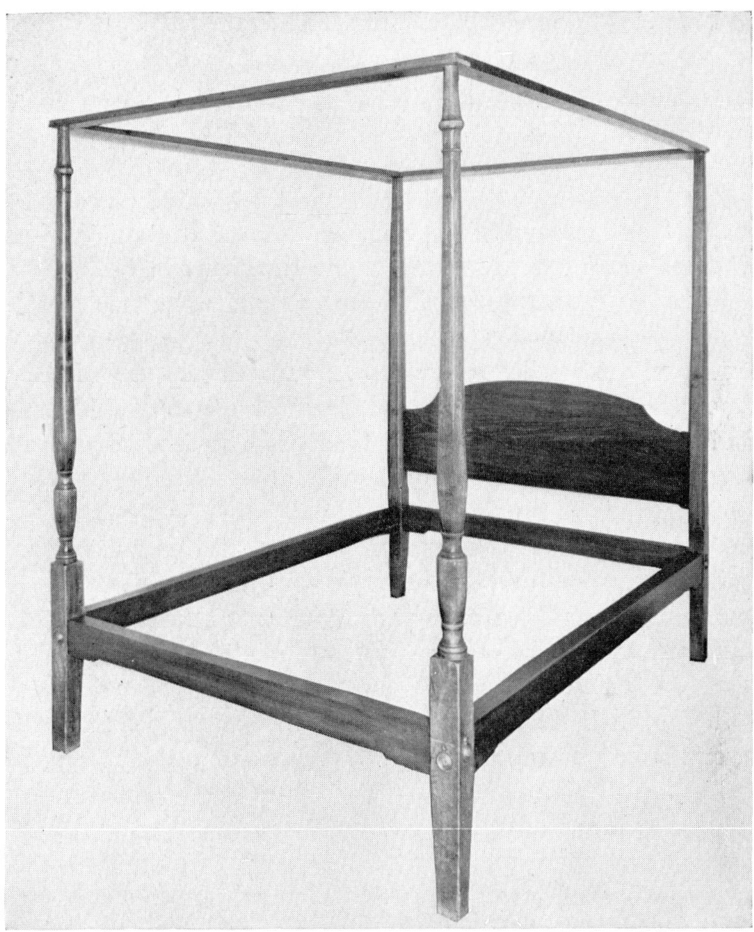

Illustration 48. *(Ginsburg & Levy, Inc.)*

A CHIPPENDALE BED

Its simplicity is characteristic of those made in America. The posts at the foot are turned. Those at the head are square and chamfered. Made 1760–1780.

Although American craftsmen under Chippendale influence carried other pieces of furniture to a high degree of excellence both in construction and in ornamental carving, beds still lagged behind. The majority were relatively simple (*Illustration 48*). For instance, the beds at Mount Vernon are of

Spartan simplicity compared with other furniture there, and yet they are of the same style-period. The one in which Washington died is just a plain frame with well-turned but unornamented uprights. No fancy shaping by ring, ball, or vase turnings, no carving, reeding, or fluting. A typical American Chippendale bed. To be sure, the posts were now turned instead of being square or eight-sided, but the tester still consisted of simple strips to support the hangings.

In England, on the contrary, beds were now most elaborate —cabriole legs, carved posts, ornamented headboards, canopy framework with a decorative cornice carved with artistic feeling of a high order. The only logical reason why the Townsend-Goddard group or the Philadelphia followers of Chippendale did not make beds of more imposing design was lack of demand. Certainly they did not lack skill or knowledge. After all, it was still a new country, given over to such dismal slogans as "The early bird catches the worm" and "Early to bed, early to rise." Beds were not places in which to dawdle over the breakfast tray and morning paper. They were useful affairs for a weary man to sleep in, even—at a sufficiently remote date —to die in. In either contingency would carving, or lack of it, on the bedposts matter.

The initial break with simplicity came about by the introduction of the tent or field bed, with its arched tester which bears a certain resemblance to the intricate canvas shelter used by officers during the Revolution when campaigning afield (*Illustration 49*). While enlisted men got along with whatever shelter they could find, a decently equipped general was housed in a tent of architectural pretensions similar to the type used at a sophisticated garden party today. Perhaps the campaigning that had gone on since Bunker Hill brought such tents to the attention of cabinetmakers and gave them the style hint or the design maybe of English origin. In any case, by 1780 Philadelphia craftsmen were making them. Whether members of the Continental Congress brought field beds home with them is not clear, but it is certain that they were soon made throughout the states to the northward and the design stayed in favor for over a generation.

The Girard estate preserves the tent bed made for Stephen Girard in Philadelphia about 1790. The posts are square from side rails to floor but turned above, and those at the foot which

Illustration 49. *(Henry Ford, Esq.)*

A FIELD BED COMPLETE WITH CANOPY

At the left is a simple cradle of the 17th Century. The bed, which is Sheraton in feeling, was made between 1795 and 1810.

would not be hidden by draperies are ornamented by the spiral or rope turnings characteristic of Sheraton. These posts have a pleasing curve and diminish in size as they near the top. The canopy frame is of the double-curve type, and there is a vase finial at each corner. Forty-five years later a cabinet-maker at Shoreham, Vermont, a farming town on Lake Champlain, made a bed so like it that if I had not seen both I should not have believed it possible. This shows the persistence of a style years after it had seemingly been discarded and makes one chary of putting an exact date on any piece. The date of a style-beginning is easily established; but how long it lasted in all parts of the country is another matter. The world was larger then, and fashions neither moved nor died as quickly as nowadays. They progressed from important centres to the rural areas, and how long they stayed current there can never be fixed exactly.

The field bed, if not of American origin, was surely developed and brought to its highest state here. In turning the upright posts, which were five or six feet tall, the old cabinetmakers gave them a delicate vase shaping. The two at the foot were further ornamented by reeding or spiral turning, and sometimes all four posts were so treated. In later examples the legs below the rails were also turned rather than left square as in earlier forms. On some, all square edges of posts and rails were refined by delicate rule-joint molding accomplished with a plane. The headboards remained relatively simple, either curved in a broad flat arch on the upper edge or sloping to a central point like a house roof. The curve of the canopy was either the well-sprung flat arch or the double curve which duplicates itself from head to foot post. Tent beds were made of mahogany, all native hardwoods, and even pine. One owned by General Stark of Revolutionary fame, has posts of curly maple and other parts of the same wood but straight grain. The Vermont bed alluded to was of cherry, and one in the author's collection acquired at Harrison, Maine, original even to the eight hand-wrought bed screws, is made of yellow birch. Some, principally rural-made, were built with side rails twenty-two to twenty-six inches from the floor, while those designed for town houses were lower, about sixteen to twenty inches from floor to mattress level.

The practice of the old cabinetmakers in canopy framework was to make each side in two pieces, hinged at the centre, crossbars lap-jointed at head and foot and others dovetailed. Other construction puts the framework under suspicion as to genuineness. The pins at top of posts that hold the arched frame should be of hand-wrought iron about an eighth of an inch in diameter. The side and end rails can be expected to be bored for the rope lattice on which the mattress rested, and most beds will be found equipped with eight screws to make the joining of rails and posts firm. All screw-holes except the two at the back of the head posts had brass rosettes to conceal the countersunk heads. For grace and pleasing lines these field beds are almost without rival among the more commonly found types of American beds, and fortunately they are not so rare that the average collector cannot aspire to own one sometime. Locating one complete in every detail is unusual good fortune. Quite often the canopy is missing, but if one is not too much of a stickler for pieces in original condition, a repair man can reproduce the missing parts when he understands what is desired.

After the field bed had demonstrated that utter simplicity in bed frames was not necessary, came those of the Hepplewhite and Sheraton periods. Those of Phyfe's best years can well be considered the outstanding examples of what he and his contemporaries could produce for those willing to pay the price. Here beauty lay in the ornamentation applied to the posts. Headboards were never intricately treated as were those of some of the finer English pieces. Either they remained severely plain, or they were given a little cresting or like finish along the upper edge. The tester, too, was generally left a simple frame from which to hang the draperies. Occasionally, as with the Derby bed by Samuel McIntire, it became a decorative cornice. In fact, this bed made for a member of that merchant prince family of Salem and now in the Boston Art Museum, probably marks the high point reached by native cabinetmakers with this type.

Such beds always had posts of mahogany. Below the rails they were either square or reeded, while above they were al-

Illustration 50. *(Gallery of Fine Arts, Yale Univ.)*

A SHERATON BED WITH DECORATED CORNICE

Made in Salem, Massachusetts, it distinctly shows workmanship characteristic of that locality. The spread-eagle ornaments on the cornice are typical of the patriotic motifs used during the first two decades of the 19th Century.

ways turned in an elongated vase shape and reeded with carving of acanthus-leaf, water-leaf, drapery, or grain-head motifs applied over this. The common practice was to lavish this beauty of detail on the foot posts and leave those at the head relatively plain. The cornice was usually of carved pine,

Illustration 51. *(Henry Ford, Esq.)*

A TYPICAL NEW ENGLAND LOW–POST BED

This type began to be made about 1820 and persisted in the back regions as late as 1850. The turnings of later examples were generally much heavier.

painted or gilded, often related in treatment to the cornice of the room for which it was designed (*Illustration 50*). Obviously beds of this type were never inexpensive, and their production was correspondingly limited. When found today they bring high prices.

It was but a step from the beds just described to those done in the American Empire manner, and the best of these was almost as fine. When the posts were delicately executed and not of too-ample cross section, they were pieces of high artistic merit. Acanthus and pineapple carving is typical as well as reeding and rope turning, while the outline of the headboard is relieved with curved volutes at the upper corners. They were made with posts of full height surmounted by a tester and also with half-high ones requiring no drapery framework. Later came the low-poster, but it is unusual to find one fabricated with lightness and delicacy (*Illustration 51*).

As the vogue for American Empire beds spread across the country, it was unfortunate that many of the cabinetmakers and turners seemed possessed with a passion for sturdiness. If slender posts were good, stout ones were better, seemed to be their philosophy. From 1820 to 1840, beds by the hundreds with posts and side rails four or five inches square were turned out. Some had posts so tall that they could only be set up in a room with abnormally high ceiling; some were of the half-high type while the majority were low-posters. Not all are clumsy. Although not delicate, a few of them have a simple dignity that must be respected. In the more elaborate examples, ornamentation of posts was achieved by a combination of turning and carving with the typical motifs of the periods employed. The posts of some of the half-high beds were decorated by vase, ring, and ball turnings that result in very pleasing effects. Carving is the exception rather than the rule with low-posters. Generally the posts are vase- and ring-turned with balls, urns, or cones providing the finish for the tops of the posts.

The earliest of American Empire beds apparently had only a headboard. Then a few were made with a footboard of the same size and shape. Next came the turned cross-member at the foot sometimes known as a blanket roll. The latter is almost always found in beds of gross proportions and so may well be considered a distinct symptom of the decadent. Low four-posters were produced for some time after the high and half-high forms were no more. They finally degenerated into the so-called spool beds, which were a factory product of no artistic merit. Why people who say they like antiques buy these knobby affairs, which are at best decadent expressions of the bamboo turnings of Sheraton influence, is hard to understand. I have never seen more than one or two examples of the spool bed possessing inherent beauty even in a dilute degree, yet how many times have I heard, "You *must* see my spool bed." For politeness' sake I have long suffered in silence, but now I say plainly, "Spool beds, as a class, are spinach. Away with them!"

Along with the three forms of the four-poster our cabinetmakers made another style that was pure, undiluted Empire. It was known as the sleigh or Napoleon bed (*Illustration 52*). Made always of solid and veneered mahogany, with its paneled head and footboards of the same height—about forty-two inches—and wide flat sidepieces, it was a direct style importation from France and mirrored the classic revival that took place there at that time. In its early form with head and footboards curving gracefully outward, it had a chaste beauty. The prevailing elephantiasis soon claimed it, however. The ends became perpendicular, and the delicate moldings were supplanted by wabbly three-level excrescences.

One important mechanical detail resulted from the production of the sleigh bed in this country. In making these for his southern clientele, John Hewitt, a New York cabinetmaker, invented a new means of holding sides and ends fast which replaced the bed screw and was the prototype for all styles of bed catches that have been developed since. (This inventive turn of mind descended to his grandson, Peter Cooper Hewitt, and produced many things, including the mercury vapor lamp.) The Napoleon bed was particularly popular in the South, and many northern cabinetmakers like Hewitt and his son Francis cultivated this market, with the result that today more of this type will be found south of Washington than north.

The crimes perpetrated on many old beds in an effort to

Illustration 52. *(Mrs. William H. P. Phyfe)*

A MAHOGANY SLEIGH BED

It was made in the Phyfe shops about 1835 and has never been out of the family.

modernize them have been legion. When the high-posters went out of fashion more than one ruthless owner amputated the posts just above the headboard to simulate the latest thing in low-posters. Such a bed tells its own story today because the turnings cease abruptly. In a genuine low-post type they would taper gracefully toward the top. Still more common was the practice in the fifties of cutting off bedposts six or eight inches from the bottom. Here again it is easily detected, as the final ring turning at the bottom will be missing.

Even today, people do not seem satisfied to leave well enough alone. There seems to be a passion abroad for cutting-over fine old beds into twin sizes. Old beds that were originally produced in pairs of something less than full width seem to be in the same class with the Indian rope trick. I have heard about them from many sources, but never have I been able to track down and see with my own eyes a pair of all-original twin beds. Single-width ones were occasionally made for small rooms or to meet special needs as the Lafayette bed at Mount Vernon. Even they are rare today, and to find two alike would be a piece of good fortune hardly probable.

So many people, apparently feeling that if the old craftsmen did not make twin beds they should have done so, proceed to correct conditions by ordering a patient repair man to make the necessary reduction in width. This cutting off a foot or so robs the beds of proportion, destroys the symmetry of the originals, and turns them into just cut-overs. So much for beds that match exactly. Even more reconstruction takes place where they are not quite alike. Here the posts of the more elaborate one are used for the foot while those of the simpler bed become the headposts. The two headboards are recut until they are duplicates and twin beds are achieved but they are now reconstructions and look it. What is more, their value has depreciated at least half. Therefore, both artistically and financially, if one must have beds of the twin variety it is better to get modern ones well reproduced from full-size originals.

There is, however, one modern adaptation for the old bed that even the most bigoted antiquarian will not cavil at, and that is substituting a spring and mattress for the old rope network and feather bed. Modern bones do not take kindly to the lumps and ridges of the latter. Happily any old bed frame can be equipped with the best 20th Century spring and mattress without reconstructing or mutilating the frame. A coil or woven wire spring that fits snugly inside the side rails, two or three strips of two-inch-wide wood, long enough to reach from side to side, screwed on the undersurface of the side rails to support the spring, and a mattress the full width of the bed frame are all that is needed. The old rope holes or pegs in the rails can be left as they are. They will be concealed by coverlet or counterpane, and if need arises will be an irrefutable evidence of genuineness. The old beds were six feet to six feet four inches in length. Some people complain that they are too short. The answer to that is new side rails of the desired length. But don't destroy the old ones. Put them away in attic or storeroom. With all the original rails and the two of extra length, the bed is worth an original price. Without the old sidepieces it is incomplete and worth correspondingly less.

Shellac or varnish was the finish for beds of mahogany, walnut, or curly maple and was often used for those of different woods. The use of paint as a furniture finish was not unknown, however, even in early days. Some of the beds of the 17th and 18th Centuries were finished with colored paints such as robin's-egg blue, rust red, and even black. By 1750 a new finish which we now call New England red filler came into vogue, and it remained popular to the end of our American Empire years. It was made of a combination of red pigment and boiling-hot sour milk and was intended to simulate mahogany. But the red was too vivid and its pigment was so dense that it obscured all traces of grain. Hence its resemblance to the popular tropical wood of the day was so slight as to deceive no one. Time has been a good friend to this raw red finish and softened it to a rather pleasing reddish brown. A bed, table, or chest found in usable condition with this finish should simply be cleaned. The mellowed New England red has its merits and, since it is a proof of genuineness, adds to the value of the piece.

CHAPTER FOUR

DESKS AND SECRETARIES

FROM the settlement of Jamestown to the close of the first quarter of the 19th Century was a golden age of letter writing and diary keeping. Captain John Smith chronicled the colonizing efforts made in Virginia; Governor William Bradford did the same for the Plymouth Plantation; Judge Sewall's journal records a wealth of everyday happenings; the Reverend Cotton Mather likewise omitted from his diary little that was going on about him. Benjamin Franklin carried on a voluminous correspondence at home and abroad and wrote his *Autobiography* for the benefit of his illegitimate son, the royalist governor of the Jerseys. Washington conducted a large if terse correspondence and left behind him a detailed journal of his conduct of the Mount Vernon estates. John and Abigail Adams by letter bridged the miles which separated them when patriotic duty detained him from home months and even years at a time. Jefferson, too, was always writing letters to express his point of view on important matters. It was a labor of love with no short cuts. The machine on which an individual might type his thoughts was far in the future, and the words "Take a letter, please" were yet unspoken. It was each man for himself with quill pen and in longhand. There was also no postal service. Nevertheless, up and down the coast and back and forth across the Atlantic, there flowed a ceaseless and ever increasing flood of letters anent business, politics, scholarly and theological interests, and family affairs. They were long and usually terminated with "Your humble and obedient servant." Goose quills by the thousands and ream after ream of handmade paper were consumed.

Obviously pieces of furniture on which to do all this writing must have existed from the start. But the early forms were not desks at all. They were, as shown in an earlier chapter, the larger chests in miniature (*Illustration 17*). Books, writing materials, and particularly treasured possessions were stored within. The flat top was the writing surface. Whether placed on a table, joined stool, or held in the lap, it was anything but a convenient arrangement. Then about 1650 some one thought of a box with a slanting lid and took the first real step toward developing that piece of furniture especially designed for writing, the desk. The first of these, save for the lid that sloped upward and away from the person using it and was hinged at the high side, was no different from the flat-lidded boxes. Then came compartments for paper, quill pens, inkpots, and sand boxes, the substitute for blotting paper until well into the 19th Century. Twenty inches from front to rear, sixteen wide, eight high at the back, and four at the front were the dimensions of a box of the slant top variety. It was provided with a lock and key, and the sides were generally ornamented with shallow carving more or less geometric in design. Still it was a writing box to be placed on a table when in use, and so its size was kept small enough for easy handling. Then it was made somewhat deeper and into the added space a drawer was introduced. The woods used for these early forms were oak for better-made ones and pine for the cruder.

The next step in the evolution was to make the box larger and rest it on a supporting frame of turned uprights and square cross-members, structurally the same as those of the early tavern table. And now we see it emerging from the polliwog stage and becoming a true desk. As our cabinet-makers continued to make these boxes on frames, they increased their size and sometimes added a drawer (*Illustration 53*). The chest, too, was developed into the chest of drawers and had its effect on desk design in two ways. A rectangular inclosed frame fitted with several drawers was substituted for the supporting frame; the slanting lid was

Illustration 53. *(Ginsburg & Levy, Inc.)*

A SLANT–TOP WRITING BOX ON FRAME

Here the late 17th Century design of the box is coupled with a very early 18th Century framework base of the tavern table type.

Illustration 54.

A DESK ON FRAME

The open writing-lid rests on two sliding brackets, and the small drawers and pigeonholes have curved outlines. A New England piece of maple with some parts of pine. *Ca.* 1720.

hinged at the bottom, and the angle of its slope increased. No more groping around in the compartments beneath for needed supplies with one hand while the clumsy lid slipped out of the other and descended with trying results on wrist and temper. The lid now folded outward and rested firmly on sliding bracket supports beneath. Thus, when the desk was open the things kept in the pigeonholes were directly before the writer and readily at hand (*Illustration 54*).

When the writing box was thus wedded to a frame and became a desk, making of these primitive forms more or less ceased until the Empire and Sheraton years. Then many small, oblong writing boxes with top and bottom separated by a slanting cut were produced. They were chiefly made of mahogany mounted with brass escutcheons, corners, and edges. They had ingenious compartments for writing supplies, correspondence, and sometimes hidden recesses for confidential memoranda and money. Lawyers who rode circuit in the first quarter of the 19th Century were partial to these latter-day variations of the Puritan Bible box. One inherited by the author from a legal great-uncle had all its interior lined with red morocco. When the lid was laid back, it exposed a slanting writing surface ten by sixteen inches with pen tray, inkpot, and sand bottle at the top. The upper half of this was hinged, and beneath was a place for writing paper and the like. Beneath the lower half of the writing surface, also hinged, was a tray of toilet articles such as razor, lance for blood letting, a glass jar holding an ounce or so of snuff and a most efficient corkscrew. Originally there was a cowhide leather case into which the box could be slipped for protection when taken on stagecoach journeys—the 1825 version of the combined brief and toilet case. Can you see a 20th Century sales manager or corporation attorney with such a writing box before him as he endeavors to continue work while aboard a limited transcontinental train or airship?

As the slant-top desk came about when the William and Mary style was in vogue, American craftsmen naturally made these pieces with the ball or turnip foot and other ornamental designs of the period (*Illustration 55*). They also continued to make their smaller desks with the framework base of the tavern table. The more elaborate had the lid hinged at the bottom, while the simpler types reverted to the earlier form and were

Illustration 55. (*Gallery of Fine Arts, Yale Univ.*)

A WILLIAM AND MARY SLANT-TOP DESK

It was made before 1720 in New England. It has burl walnut veneer on drawer fronts and lid.

hinged at the top. Some had a drawer inserted in the upper section; others were made with a second one located in the top of the supporting frame. Craftsmen showed that they realized they were combining the old writing box with a frame base, for they made them separate. In an emergency the piece could become dual-purpose by removing the upper box and substituting a table top. This primitive desk design persisted longer than is commonly realized. With lid hinged either at top or at bottom, but more frequently the former, it was the model for a long

Illustration 56. (*Author's collection*)

A SIMPLE PINE SCHOOLMASTER'S DESK

A rural piece that may have been made as late as 1840. The tapered legs are Hepplewhite in feeling but lack delicacy.

line of schoolmaster's and countinghouse desks all through the 18th and the first half of the 19th Century. The various style periods affected it slightly both ornamentally and structurally, and toward the last it was made in a single piece rather than in two parts (*Illustration 56*).

Illustration 57. (*Gallery of Fine Arts, Yale Univ.*)

A COUNTRY-MADE QUEEN ANNE DESK

Here the base is separate from the top as with some of the chests and chests of drawers of the period. The pendent finials of the apron seem to be a survival from the William and Mary lowboys. *Ca.* 1720–1730.

During the Queen Anne years, desks were principally made with a frame base similar to that used with chests of drawers. Here either short turned legs ending in button feet or longer cabriole legs with the Dutch foot were used in place of the trestle taken over from the tavern table. Sometimes the horizontal pieces connecting these legs at the upper ends—there never were any cross-members near the floor with Queen Anne desks or chests of drawers—were cut in valance lines to provide that characteristic ornamental apron. Within the upper part the simple partitioning which formed the pigeonholes of earlier days was replaced by more elaborate work, and a number of small drawers added (*Illustration 57*). This was to reach its high point during the Chippendale years to follow. Then came a multiplicity of compartments and often secret ones skillfully concealed. As a usual thing these hiding places are located behind the central section or on either side of it. With the latter, a pilaster of the split banister form ornaments the front of a tall, deep, but thin drawer called a document box. A pin or peg that is released by finger pressure is the usual manner of holding the concealed containers that flank the central section (*Illustration 58*). To locate the releases, feel carefully for the button or pin. With the former a slight pressure will release the compartment as it generally has a wooden spring at the back which forces the whole container out a little when the retaining button is depressed. With the pin type, simply pull out the pin. When the secret space is behind the centre section, there are usually two small, thin wooden bolts, one on either side, that hold it firm and can be released by sliding inward. Usually such catches have a little depression in their outer surface into which the tip of the forefinger fits naturally.

These secret compartments are a fitting rival to the buried treasure of Captain Kidd for the false hopes they raise in the human breast. Repair men refinishing desks so tricked out always hope to run across pine-tree shillings, valuable letters or signatures, Continental paper currency, or original documents. Always they are disappointed. It is apparent that the original owners of such desks did not highly regard their secret spots as places of safety and seclusion. Nevertheless, there is an interesting air of mystery about them, and in their making the old cabinetmakers frequently did very fine work, which of itself materially increases the value of a piece.

Under the influence of the Chippendale style American craftsmen adhered closely to the design and structural plan they utilized in making chests of drawers. Most of the desks had four drawers, a slanting front that rested on sliding arms

Illustration 58. *(C. Sanford Bull, Esq.)*

A CONNECTICUT DESK OF ABOUT 1750

The legs, feet and apron are Queen Anne in feeling, but the blocking of drawer-fronts and interior show Chippendale characteristics. A transitional piece.

or brackets, and either short cabriole legs terminating in claw-and-ball feet or bracket feet which might or might not be developed with molding elements on the outer surfaces. Two features marked these desks. The first was the wealth of ornamental detail and fine workmanship lavished on the pigeon-hole compartments in contrast to the simple interiors of the two preceding style periods. The second feature was the addition of an upper or bookcase section. This caused the piece to take on such imposing proportions that the simple Anglo-Saxon term "desk" seemed quite inadequate. So from the French *escritoire* was derived the well-rounded, sonorous word "secretary." A distinction without a difference, and a choice morsel for philologists. In short, take off its dignified headpiece, and it is a desk; put it on, and it is a secretary.

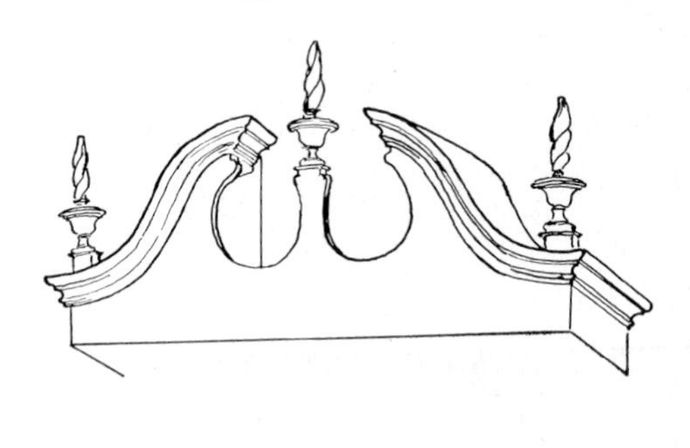

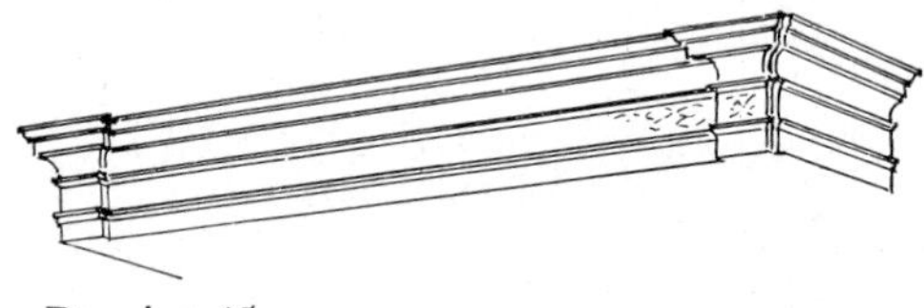

Drawing 15.

BONNET-TOP AND FLAT CORNICE COMPARED

Such treatment was used with secretaries and highboys.

The upper sections made at this time were provided with paneled doors and either a bonnet top similar to that of the highboys or a fine cornice in which nice molding and finely executed dentelations were used (*Drawing 15*). The John Goddard secretaries which he made about 1760 for the brothers Brown, outstanding merchant princes of Providence, are ultimate specimens. They are practically identical. The base is block-fronted with shell carving like the typical Goddard-Townsend chests of drawers. This design is carried out on the outer surface of the slanting lid and in the upper section, where the front is made of three panels, the outer ones being in relief and the centre one again incised. In the interior the effect of the block-fronts and shell-carved lunettes

Illustration 59. *(Gallery of Fine Arts, Yale Univ.)*

A CHIPPENDALE SECRETARY

It was made by John Goddard of Newport, Rhode Island. The raised and incised shell carvings are typical of the Rhode Island group of craftsmen, as is the block-front treatment of the drawers. Goddard's working years were 1740–1790. This desk antedates 1775.

is continued by a centre compartment and others at the extreme right and left in which the drawer-fronts are shaped to balance in reverse the recessed door of the central compartment. Between these on either side there are groups of three pigeon-holes, each with a shallow shell carving at the top. The broken pediment of the bonnet top is executed in graceful cyma curves with an arched cornice molding. At the centre and outer curves there are three carved finials of the conventionalized flame type (*Illustration 59*).

Other fine secretaries were made by cabinetmakers in New England and Philadelphia. Some had block fronts; others, the various forms of the serpentine, and occasionally one was straight. Either the flat or the bonnet top was used, but a pair of paneled doors was the rule rather than Goddard's triple arrangement. The interior of the upper part was always divided into a number of compartments of varying sizes for account books, important papers, and the like, thus forming the filing cabinet of the day. On the sides of the lower section and occasionally the upper as well, large brass drop handles were mounted, showing their makers had not forgotten the origin of such pieces and subconsciously added these trappings of the earlier great chest (*Illustration 58*).

The knee-hole desk, that type with a flat top and, as its name suggests, a recessed centre in the base flanked on either side by tiers of drawers the full depth of the piece, was first made in England during the William and Mary period. It did not make its American début until the Chippendale era, and even then was seldom produced. Hence American desks of this type are extremely rare (*Illustration 60*). The Townsend-Goddard group made a few in which they exercised their fondness for the block front. This design fitted the knee-hole type well, and the recessed centre cupboard accentuated it. A few others were made by Philadelphia craftsmen in either mahogany or walnut, but nearly all desks of this sort offered for sale today are of English origin. Those of American make, because of their rarity, are museum pieces and command corresponding prices.

The most popular and satisfactory desk form of all was undoubtedly the regular slant-top with four drawers below already referred to. They were made with block, serpentine, or

Illustration 60. *(Gallery of Fine Arts, Yale Univ.)*

A KNEE-HOLE DESK

Also made by Goddard, and of the same decade as Illustration 59.

straight front, had either bracket or claw-and-ball feet and were produced in mahogany, walnut, cherry, plain and fancy grained maple, and even pine. Cabinetmakers of all sections kept to this design for ten or twenty years after the close of the Chippendale period. Some have imposing interiors in which centre cupboard, document boxes, and flanking pigeonholes and drawers are ornamented with shell lunettes, scalloped edges, and half-round pilasters. At the top of each pigeon-hole division a small, valance-shaped crosspiece serving as the

Illustration 61. *(Ginsburg & Levy, Inc.)*

A HEPPLEWHITE SECRETARY WITH TAMBOUR FRONT. *Ca.* 1790
Boston cabinetmakers excelled in the use of this flexible tambour work.

front of a shallow, inconspicuous drawer was frequently used. As the Hepplewhite influence made itself felt, curly maple became a favorite wood, and an inlay design ornamented the slant top. So practical was this desk form that it did not give way entirely when the Hepplewhite and Sheraton styles had gained the centre of the stage. Modified in ornamentation and minor details, it persisted even through the succeeding Empire years. Interiors, however, became simpler and seldom contained any secret compartments.

The Hepplewhite period brought with it a new design of secretary, that with the tambour front—which, being interpreted, is finely reeded woodwork mounted on a heavy linen. This flexible arrangement slides back and forth in grooves that may be bent at an angle even as sharp as ninety degrees. A very beautiful detail in the days of its creator, a most atrocious one in the roll-top of a century later. But where the latter-day abominations had flexible woodwork with the lines of ribbing horizontal, those of American Hepplewhite were always vertical. These tambour secretaries were classically simple of line. Tapered legs with their outline continued up to the writing level; one, two, or three drawers of full width, but never descending as near to the floor as with the Chippendale style; a narrow writing-leaf that rested flat when closed; a low upper section with a central closet and a pair of tambour slides serving as doors were the structural features (*Illustration 61*). The one bearing the label of John Seymour & Son referred to earlier is a remarkable piece because of the fineness of its execution. It was mahogany and had a wealth of inlaid ornamentation, of which the finest was the husk festoons that decorated the two parts of the sliding front in the upper section. In this particular piece there was no central cabinet with door dividing the shutters, which was unusual.

Hepplewhite secretaries were also made with an upper section that had doors. Both types were less formidable and more intimate than those of the Chippendale days. They were never much over six feet in height and correspondingly proportioned otherwise. When there were doors, they were usually made with glass panels set in wooden bar moldings. A typical door of this period would have three panels, each terminating in a Gothic arch. More unusual and probably of country make is the same secretary with solid doors. Here fine crotch-grain mahogany veneer was usual, and the centre of each door had an ornamental medallion of an urn or other classic design. The top was usually finished with a cornice

Illustration 62. *(Dr. George P. Coopernail)*

A HEPPLEWHITE SLANT-TOP DESK

The inlay, splayed feet and shaped apron are characteristic. Made at New Berlin, New York, after 1800 by Lewis Winslow for his own use.

made of flat members that from the outer finial blocks curved upward to a central pediment block on which frequently rested a gilded eagle with wings outspread—a patriotic touch that combined well with the classic simplicity the brothers Adam introduced to Englishmen and their American cousins.

When working in the Hepplewhite manner on the slant-top desk of the Chippendale era, our cabinetmakers replaced the bracket or claw-and-ball feet with those having the outward splay used with the chest of drawers, and incorporated a similar curved skirt connecting the feet (*Illustration 62*). Pencil-line, herring-bone, and more elaborate forms of inlay outlined the drawer fronts and the upper side of the lid. In addition, inlaid medallions were sometimes placed in the centre of the flap and that of upper drawers.

Another variety of desk was the drop-front. Here the writing compartment was drawerlike and pulled out for use. The front was hinged on the lower edge and supported with two curved brass brackets. This type was first employed in England during the Chippendale period, but with rare exceptions was not used by American craftsmen until they were making pieces of Hepplewhite design (*Illustration 63A*). The fall-front is a most ingenious plan for providing writing space in pieces not necessarily designed as desks. A drawer front is hinged at the bottom and, when the section is pulled out about half its depth, folds down and provides an excellent area for penmanship. The back third of the section is given over to drawers and compartments made along the lines of other desks. Sometimes this drawerlike writing compartment was built into a sideboard of the period, replacing the upper drawer of the centre (*Illustration 63B*). It was then known as a butler's desk on the theory that here household accounts were kept by the major-domo of a family opulent enough to afford such a dignitary. Again it might be a fine chest-on-chest with the upper drawer of the lower section replaced by such an arrangement. The old dual-purpose instinct of the 17th Century rising again.

American craftsmen again lagged behind their English brethren in the matter of break-front secretaries. While there were plenty in the Chippendale and Hepplewhite styles in the old country, the Sheraton influence was in full force before many were made here. On account of their size and cost they

Illustration 63 A. *(American Art Assn.–Anderson Galleries)*

FALL FRONT SECRETARY

Serpentine-front secretary of mahogany with solid doors. There is much Chippendale feeling in the design of this piece. Made 1770–90.

Illustration 63 B. *(Gallery of Fine Arts, Yale Univ.)*

FALL FRONT SECRETARY

Hepplewhite butler's secretary with typical oval lines of light-colored inlay contrasting with the crotch mahogany veneer. Made about 1800.

Illustration 64. *(Ginsburg & Levy, Inc.)*

A BREAK-FRONT SECRETARY

The upper drawer of the centre section is a fall-front desk compartment. Inlay and veneer are Hepplewhite in feeling and execution. Made between 1785 and 1795. It is from Salem, Massachusetts.

were never widely made in America. In fact, it is probable they were only produced on special order of dimensions proper for a particular location. Occasionally they are found with some Hepplewhite detail, but even then the Sheraton influence so predominates that it is safer to place them in the latter period (*Illustration 64*). In construction the break-front is really a fall-front with upper section flanked on either side by added bookcase, drawer, and closet compartments that are a little shallower so that the secretary section projects from four to six inches and dominates the piece. This difference in depth of centre and side parts is of course the feature that gives the name. Such secretaries were usually about eight feet tall and from six to eight wide. The doors of the upper part have panes of glass cut in diamond and other geometric shapes. Being always important pieces, they were made of mahogany, and fine crotch veneer ornamented the drawer and lower door-fronts. There was a curved cornice at the top with four finials and sometimes the gilded eagle mounted on the central pediment block. For ease in moving, these huge pieces were always made in sections.

Just as the Hepplewhite influence produced the tambour front, so under Sheraton came the barrel- or cylinder-front. The two ideas were combined in the last days of the 19th Century, and the clumsy roll-top desk already alluded to was the result. Its chief merit was its short life. In the Sheraton barrel-front the sloping lid of former periods was replaced by a quarter-round cover that rotated on its axis into the back of the case when the secretary was opened for use. This curved area was finished with well-marked mahogany veneer, and usually the piece had reeded legs of about fifteen inches. The upper part had doors with glass panels generally cut with Gothic arched tops (*Illustration 65*). Phyfe and some of the other urban cabinetmakers made secretaries of this design, but craftsmen in country communities seem to have adhered to those which were fundamentally Chippendale in construction (*Illustration 66*). Sometimes they added Sheraton touches such as the reeded leg and the shallow pilaster. Where, in chests of drawers, legs that were all but detached from the case were popular as was the bow front, these features

Illustration 65. *(Museum of the City of New York)*

A BARREL-FRONT DESK

Usually these were made in the Sheraton rather than the Hepplewhite style. Formerly owned by Alexander Hamilton. *Ca.* 1790.

were not carried over into desk and secretary making. In some of the secretaries the upper section had paneled doors and a simple broken pediment top, while the lower one had a fall-front writing section and a large closet with double doors beneath. The whole was supported by simple and fairly low bracket feet.

With the end of the Sheraton period, the well-designed desk may be said to cease. This hapless piece perhaps suffered more than any other at the hands of the American Empire en-

Illustration 66. *(Ginsburg & Levy, Inc.)*

A CURLY MAPLE DESK

Probably made after the close of the Chippendale period but closely following that style. A rural post-Revolutionary piece.

thusiasts. Secretaries now became mere ceiling scrapers, eight or nine feet tall with towering bookcase sections that threw the lower half entirely out of proportion. They were made of mahogany and sometimes rosewood; but beautiful wood is not enough, so it is better to pass such pieces by and wait for an earlier example.

For places of public meeting yet another type of desk, the flat-top of impressive dimensions, was made by American craftsmen from the Chippendale years through those of Sheraton, generally with eight legs and an open section in the centre of the base. Present-day furniture makers seem to have followed this style in producing what they unctuously call the executive desk. Consciously or not, they are indirectly copying the most historic American desks.

On the morning of July 4, 1776, in the Council Chamber of what is now Independence Hall, a document lay on a handsome flat-top desk awaiting the signature of John Hancock and the other delegates to the Continental Congress which announced to the world in general that thirteen American colonies had forsaken the political bed and board of his Britannic Majesty for, to them, good and sufficient reasons therein enumerated. The desk is still preserved in that historic building in Philadelphia, and aside from its political significance is a fine example of the restrained skill of an unknown craftsman in that city.

When the Federal government was for a brief period located in New York, that city's venerable Statehouse was given a new front, refurbished, and renamed Federal Hall. Among the pieces of new furniture—$50,000 was provided for these changes—was a presidential desk. It is now to be seen in the Governor's Room in the City Hall. There is a touch of Sheraton to the design, but fundamentally it is closely akin to the one in Philadelphia; and both are amply designed for their use, a desk at which an official might sit and transact his public business. No pigeonholes in which important papers might be mislaid. Just an expanse of top supported by two tiers of drawers on either side. Then as now, it was an efficient piece of furniture for a man of affairs.

CHAPTER FIVE

TWO CENTURIES OF CHAIRS

ONLY in the word "chairman" does there survive something of the importance and grandeur that once attached itself to one who sat in a piece of furniture that had back and arms. When the President of the United States confers in cabinet meeting with his chief administrative lieutenants, capacious chairs neatly done in leather and mahogany are provided for all. Save for name plates they do not differ. Could the scene be moved back three hundred years, the President would still have a chair, archiepiscopal in form and dignity, but all the others from the Secretary of State down would sit on backless and armless joined stools.

Chairs were few and far between prior to the last quarter of the 17th Century, and only the most important people expected them either at public gatherings or in the home. It was good for lesser men, women, and children not to be too comfortable in this transitory world. Sitting on joined stools kept their backs strong and straight and developed the sturdiness of spine so admirably reflected in their character. It also enhanced the dignity of the presiding elder. Dogelike he sat in an imposing oaken chair, substantial of frame and Tudor of ornament like an individual choir stall. It had a plain, flat board seat, painfully hard to moderns accustomed to springs and cushions; but this again was eminently suitable since the chair was not designed for comfort but as a mark of distinction, and for the good of his soul even an elder must not allow himself to be lapped in ease.

In private collections and in the more fortunate museums are preserved rare specimens of these massive wainscot chairs

Illustration 67. *(Bowdoin College)*

A 17TH CENTURY ENGLISH WAINSCOT CHAIR

With its elaborate carving, this is typical of the few fine pieces brought from England which in a measure served as models for some of the more elaborate pieces made in America during the Puritan period. This chair is credited with being made in England in 1630 and arriving in America about 1635.

in use during the first half-century of the white occupation of our North Atlantic coast. From the Governor Edward Winslow piece in Pilgrim Hall, Plymouth, which is the simplest and probably the earliest, to the elaborate chairs in the Metropolitan Museum, Essex Institute, and other collections, all follow the same plan of construction and ornamentation: a stout underbody with the front posts (they are too ample to be termed legs) turned, substantial cross-stretchers at top and bottom, plain board seat, arms curving downward slightly from the back and almost of belaying-pin size, and the back itself covered with an elaborate design not too deeply incised. These backs, like woodwork used for room walls, were constructed of panelwork framed by stiles and rails. Hence the name "wainscot chair." In them the carved design flowed nicely from the central panel to the surrounding frame, and at the top a carved cresting completed the ornamentation, some suggestion of which was also applied to the front cross-stretcher immediately beneath the seat. Like all work of the Tudor era, the design of carving is a combination of the geometric and the conventionalized.

One would look far to find a more impressive chair form for official occasions. Had some one seen fit to present one to our Federal government for use at inaugurations, the United States would have a presidential throne that would look its part. Bowdoin College has such a one. In 1872 the alma mater of Nathaniel Hawthorne was given a wainscot chair in remarkably fine condition, and since then, each June, when diplomas are dispensed to seniors in the presence of trustees, faculty, and adoring parents, the president occupies it as an academic throne (*Illustration 67*). A silver label attached states that this particular chair "made in 1630, was brought from England probably about 1635 by the ancestors of the Dennis Family of Ipswich, Massachusetts. Presented to Bowdoin College by E. W. Farley of Newcastle, Maine, June, 1872."

The earliest stools for seating lesser people were practically miniatures of the crude first tables. Simply a plank seat into which four tapering octagon legs were fitted and given an outward splay to make the stool stand firmly. The top, which was eighteen or twenty inches from the floor, was sometimes of pine and the legs of hard wood. Reduced in size still further so that it was six to eight inches tall, it became a foot stool, a most useful article in the drafty early houses. The immediate successor to these rude pieces was the joined stool (*Drawing 16*).

The term "joined" designates furniture put together with mortise and tenon joints made fast with dowel pins, and since the early craftsmen built their furniture thus they were usually known as "joyners," or later "joiners." Savery, an outstanding Philadelphia disciple of Chippendale, styled himself in his labels "joiner" rather than "cabinetmaker." The first years that Duncan Phyfe worked in New York he was listed in the city directory as a "joiner." When he changed the spelling of his name from Fife to the more Hellenic form Phyfe, he adopted "cabinetmaker" as his trade designation. Perhaps there was more balance in this. One thing is certain it was "Fife, joiner" and "Phyfe, cabinetmaker."

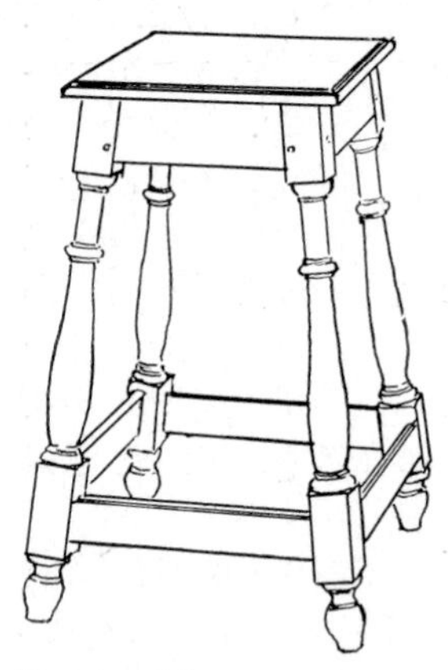

Drawing 16.

A 17TH CENTURY JOINED STOOL

In design and construction, the joined stool was a transplanted English piece. Four turned legs that splayed outward in either two or four directions, plain rectangular stretchers at top and bottom, and an oblong top generally finished with a thumb-nail molding. Structurally it was like the early tavern tables and undoubtedly the inspiration for them. The only difference was one of dimensions. This joined stool of the 17th Century makes an excellent coffee table today. In America it was made of oak, maple, or birch, but the top or seat was frequently of pine. In England, on the other hand, it was made entirely of oak, a detail well to remember since native joined stools are rare indeed and sometimes a genuine one of English origin will be offered as of native make. There is nothing wrong with these stools, but it is too bad to pay the high price for a rare American piece and receive a much commoner English one.

During the brief episode of Oliver Cromwell the idea of a little more comfort in the home gained acceptance among the common people in England. In the jargon of the 20th Century, people on both sides of the Atlantic became chair-conscious; and to meet the demand the turned chair was produced in a number of designs. Sometimes these are referred to as "thrown" chairs. This does not mean that they were handy to hurl at an obstinate spouse, it was simply a trade term for all woodwork shaped on a lathe. It still survives in certain branches of the textile trades, where "thrown silk" means material made of thread built up by twisting filaments tightly together. These chairs from the lathe, produced with only a fraction of the labor needed for even the plainest wainscot type, were by no means new. They were antique even in 1650 and originated in Constantinople when St. Sophia was a Christian basilica and not a Mohammedan mosque. The Scandinavian mercenaries who served under the Byzantine Emperors brought this chair form home. Thence it made its way into England, producing, in the Elizabethan years, the three-cornered Varangian type with a multiplicity of big and little turned spindles.

The American version of the chair form that had traveled indirectly from the Golden Horn to England, was at first made in two styles and named for two of the outstanding men of Pilgrim Plymouth. The simpler is known as the Carver (*Drawing 17*). Governor Carver's chair, preserved in Pilgrim Hall, has four turned uprights relieved with just a touch of ring turning. Those of the back terminate with nicely executed finials formed by three ball-turnings of diminishing size. The front legs seem to have had no finial ornamental finish, or else it has been worn away through the years. The back is fashioned by two cross-rungs set close together just below the finials and another about six inches from the seat. Into these are fixed three vertical spindles finished with simple ring-and-ball

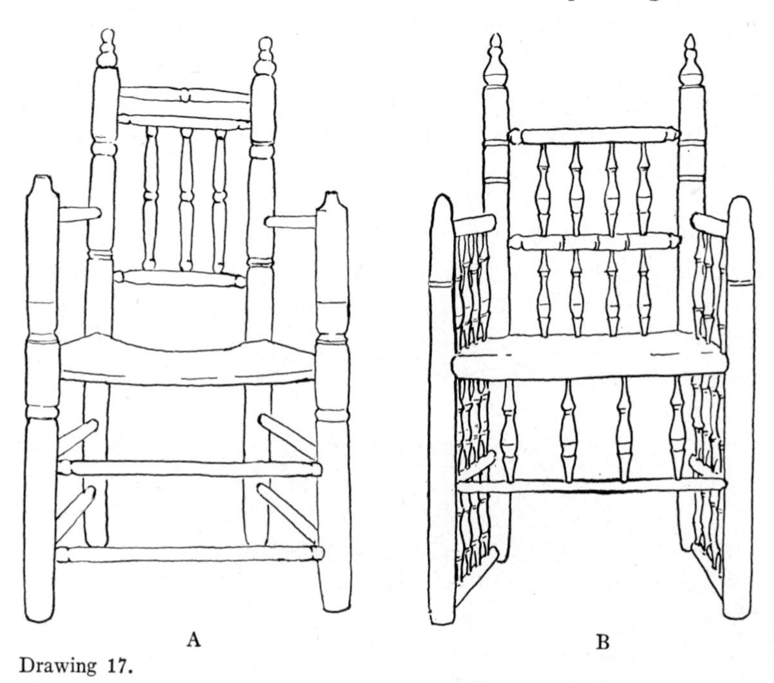

Drawing 17.

PURITAN CENTURY TURNED CHAIRS

A, the Carver; B, the Elder Brewster chair. Both were made about 1650 and are now in Pilgrim Hall at Plymouth, Massachusetts.

turnings. The arms are plain rounds connecting front and back uprights and socketed into them. The underbody has double tiers of turned stretchers or rungs at front and sides but none at the back. The uprights are substantial. They are turned from wood at least two and one-half inches square and are not finished with any ornamentation unless they, too, have disappeared through use. The original seat may have been board, rush, or splint.

The Elder Brewster chair is an elaboration of this plainer type and probably a little later (*Drawing 17*). It has the same sort of uprights and arms but differs distinctly in back and sides, where double tiers of small baluster-turned spindles are employed. In the back are three cross-rungs, one a little below the finials, another at the seat level, and the third halfway between. Fixed into these, in rows of four, are two tiers of the same small spindles. Three tiers of spindles in a like arrangement form the sides. They extend from the arms to cross-rungs that practically rest on the floor, producing a grill-like effect. The seat is a plain shaped board, and beneath it in front a skirt or valance is achieved by a plain cross-rung and four more of the vertical small spindles. In all, the maker of the Brewster chair used thirty-six baluster-turned short spindles, and the final effect is so complicated as to be in itself an explanation why, during the period, more of the simpler Carver pattern were made.

Whether to consider these two as different types or as simply variations of the Byzantine theme is an academic question. In either case, it is from them that the long line of rod, banister, and slat-back chairs descended. They were made for nearly two centuries by American "throwers," first in the older settlements and then in the newer and remote farming villages as far south as the Tennessee River and westward into the Ohio Valley. In fact, even today in the common porch chair with either rattan or slats for seat and back, may be found the old, old style in a degenerate form.

Since slat-back chairs of distinctly 17th Century workmanship are not excessively rare, it is reasonable to suppose they were contemporaries of the Carver and Brewster types. Here the turned uprights were of the same generous diameter and the ornamentation by finials and ring turnings definitely of that period. The slats were either three or four in number and wider than those used later. From side to side they curved backward, and where the ends were mortised into the back-posts a quarter-circle cut reduced the width of the slat nearly half. In addition the upper and lower edges were straight in contrast to the arched or curved types of the 18th and 19th Centuries (*Drawing 18*). The arms remained plain rounds socketed into the front and back uprights a little below the large knob or button turnings that terminated the upper ends of the front pair. Toward the close of the century these arms took on minor refinements, such as being somewhat flattened and elliptical of cross section or even shaped like those of the wainscot variety. That is, the front ends overlapped the uprights, which were socketed into them dowel-like (*Illustration 68*). The underbody treatment remained severely plain. Possibly, a suggestion of ring-turning on the front uprights, but more often no ornamental relief at all. The stretchers were rounds about the diameter of a broom handle. If there were any feet, they were probably of the button type and, to judge by surviving examples, either they never existed or they have disappeared through the wear and tear of time.

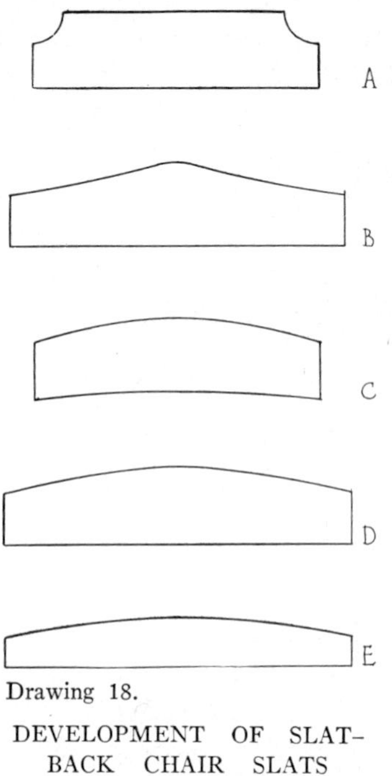

Drawing 18.

DEVELOPMENT OF SLAT-BACK CHAIR SLATS

A, 17th Century; B, early 18th; C, late 18th; D, early 19th; E, later 19th Century.

With the 18th and 19th Centuries came ball-and-vase stretchers as well as feet related to the ring-, ball-, and vase-turnings of both front and rear uprights. With some, the round arms of the 17th Century continued to be used with an element of fancy turning at the centre to relieve the plainness. The turned uprights were also made lighter, and the finials of those at the back had many shapes (*Drawing 19*). Knobs, egg-shaped ovals, and urns were most often used. In

Illustration 68. *(Gallery of Fine Arts, Yale Univ.)*

AN EARLY 18TH CENTURY SLAT-BACK CHAIR

The five slats are of descending width, and the shaping of arms and turnings of uprights are characteristic of work before 1750.

design and proportions of slats can be found very reliable indications of the approximate time of making. Those five or even six inches wide, the upper one perhaps the widest and the others graduating downward with upper and lower edges straight, can safely be considered as 17th Century work. After that, the trend was to make slats three to four and one-half inches wide and give the upper edges an arclike curve. The lower edges were usually left straight. In very sophisticated, urban-produced chairs such as one bearing the Savery label, a triple curve was employed. The 19th Century brought

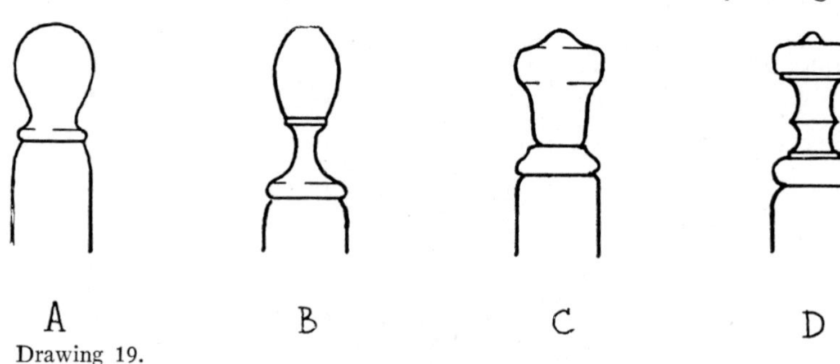

Drawing 19.

TYPICAL 18TH AND 19TH CENTURY SLAT-BACK CHAIR FINIALS

A, simple knob; B, egg-shaped knob; C and D, simple and elaborate urns.

still narrower slats. Two and a half to three and a half inches was the average width. Also in these latter chairs there was a tendency to fashion the arms flat horizontally but with an outward flare from back to front. The fronts of the arms generally had a volute finish, and the ends of the front uprights were socketed into them. Also the uprights were lighter, an inch and a half being the diameter of many.

To form a sufficient concave curve to be comfortable for the human back, slats were either steamed or soaked until pliable. This curve was sometimes as much as two inches in depth though about an inch and a quarter was more usual. They were made of ash, oak, and various other hard woods, as were the uprights, arms, and stretchers. Ash was the favorite with 17th Century craftsmen because it was plentiful and turned readily on their foot- or water-power lathes. During this century, chairs were made with only three or at most four slats because of the width of the latter. In the 18th and 19th Centuries four slats were the rule, although in rare instances, five were used. There is a chair with five slats now in the collection of the Pennsylvania Historical Society which was once owned by William Penn. When he was preparing to make his home in Penn's Woods, New World, he sent ahead a cabinetmaker from Holland and wrote his agent specifically about the furniture this man was to make. Perhaps the quintation of slats came from the hands of the indentured Hollander. On one arm of this particular chair is carved a bit of doggerel with a distinct *Poor Richard's Almanac* flavor:

I know not where
I know not when
But in this chair
Sat William Penn

If Benjamin did write this to spoof the good people of Philadelphia for Pennolatry, time has evened the score. One of the proudest possessions of Columbia University is a mahogany armchair of the Chippendale years upholstered in black haircloth. In the trustees' room it stands at the head of the conference table, and on its back is a silver plaque telling those who would read that it was once the library chair of *Doctor* Benjamin Franklin and was bequeathed to Columbia by his son-in-law, Simon Bache.

Since slats in the old types were only three-sixteenths to a quarter of an inch thick, a chair bearing those of thicker wood is probably either a clumsily made one of the very last years or a modern reproduction. Sharp edges are also an indication of recent fabrication. These chairs were made both with and without arms. Producing them as side or "lady" chairs began at the end of the first quarter of the 18th Century and continued to the closing days of slat-back chair production in the rural communities, which was doubtless about 1825 at the latest. After that, country chair makers turned to the painted "fancy," of which those by Hitchcock, made at Riverton, Connecticut, in great numbers with rush, cane, or solid wooden seats are the outstanding example.

The turned feet on most old slat-back chairs are missing and in such a case the lower rungs are within an inch of the floor (*Illustration 8*). Somebody was old and wanted a nice, comfortable low chair with a back that sloped backward a bit. That was easy. Just cut the feet from an old slat-back, and do it so that the back uprights would be a trifle shorter than the front. Or perhaps there was not quite money enough in the ginger jar for one of those newfangled rocking chairs so soothing and comfortable. Amputate the feet of a faithful old slat-back and replace them with rockers. So, today, the collector as a rule has to be content with chairs that are footless or have a skilled repair man replace the simple turnings by splicing so they will not come loose or the restoration be noticeable.

Sometimes chairs of this type were made in sets with an armchair for father and side ones for the rest of the family. Unfortunately, time, family partitions, and various movings from old to new homes have separated them so completely that finding a set intact is most unusual. Even as late as 1910 slatbacks were so little regarded by Americans as a class that they were jettisoned without qualms, while graceless chairs of the late Empire and early black walnut eras were preserved with infinite pains.

My own grandfather refused point-blank to let me preserve such a set that had been made in New Hampshire about 1790. Instead with pride and satisfaction he covered and crated an upholstered monstrosity of the early Victorian period that in form was prophetic of the Good Queen's own figure in her last years.

The rod-back, which takes its name from the vertical turned

uprights forming the back, was directly related to the Carver chair. It was made in both arm and side chairs during the rest of the 17th Century and through most of the 18th, but did not survive to see the colonies converted by force of flintlocks and brass cannon into a sovereign and separate political entity.

Speaking genealogically of the banister-back, one can properly say its parents were the Carver-Brewster and the carved and crested Carolean chairs. Certainly its frame is the former while its proportions and ornamentation distinctly favor the latter. So few of the Carolean type were made here that, interesting as they are to specialists, they may be dismissed with a bare mention of their elaborate Flemish scrolls and seat and back panel of woven cane—a material that reached England from India via Portugal during the Restoration. This is also true of an earlier type, the Cromwellian chair, that had a square and turned underbody which in design was a direct borrowing from the Continent. The upper panel and seat of this chair were upholstered either with leather or with a textile. Both styles were widely made in England. In America their place was taken either by joined stools or by chairs of the Carver-Brewster design.

The banister-back came into vogue about the end of the William and Mary period and continued in popularity for about fifty years (*Illustration 69*). Its name, of course, came from the treatment of the uprights of the back, and, while occasionally employed in provincial English pieces, it was primarily an American achievement. From a carved and crested or shaped upper crosspiece to a simple one a little above the seat, four or five vertical slats provided the back. They were flat on the front side and half-round on the back like the spindles beneath the handrail of a stairway only split vertically. The shaping of half-round slats was varied, but essentially all were vase-and-ball turnings. These chairs were made with and without arms. The rear uprights were usually square from the seat level down, and above were turned in vase, ring-and-ball de-

Illustration 69.

A BANISTER–BACK CHAIR

The sunburst carved crest of the top is unusual. The turned front, feet, and stretchers are in unusually fine condition. Of New England origin. *Ca.* 1725.

signs except for short distances where the upper and lower crosspieces of the back were mortised into them. There they were square and of the same size as the leg part. The front uprights were turned in like manner but, unlike the rear ones, were provided with feet. They might be simple buttons, turnips, or the carved Spanish type sometimes carried over to the Queen Anne cabriole leg to replace the simpler duck foot. The front and side stretchers were nearly always ornamentally turned. Many had but one front cross-member which was turned in bold relief. Two ball or melon elements separated by a ring or collar were a popular treatment for this single stretcher, which was placed halfway between the seat-level and the floor. Those at the side, while not plain, were never so deeply turned and were, as a rule, simple vase-shapings. There were usually two on each side. The back stretcher, being out of sight, was perfectly plain. Were there arms, they were shaped with a slight downward curve from the back forward, and at the outer ends carved knuckles which curved both outward and downward were a favorite treatment. Sometimes these were given added finish by grooves that were continuous from back to under surfaces of the knuckles. The seats were always of twisted rush, and the upper crosspiece of the back, if not carved, had the cresting effect produced by scroll-saw cutting. Usually this was a combination of curves and arches culminating with one or two central ones noticeably higher than the rest. With some New England chairs a pair of conventionalized fish tails were worked into the cresting.

Maple was the most popular wood for banister-backs although other hard woods with a straight grain were used, and these chairs were made in quantity in all of the colonies as far south as Pennsylvania and possibly Maryland and Virginia. From 1700 to about 1730 was their heyday, although simpler ones were produced much later in remote hill-towns of New England. From its advent to its last years, the finish was almost universally paint. Dark red, bottle-green, and black were the popular colors. No active hues to lend a color note to a room. A few were turned out with a reddish brown graining intended to simulate walnut, which was then popular. Fewer still were those made with curly-grained split-banisters, arms, and ornamental cross-stretchers that must have been finished in varnish.

When the banister-back was at the height of its popularity, there developed in southern New England a variation of it that foretold the coming Queen Anne chair with fiddle back and cabriole leg. Here the split-banister uprights were displaced by a single central splat that in silhouette was so like the outline of a violin as to earn for it the name "fiddle-back." Actually this is a misnomer, since the shaping of the piece was inspired not by the musical instrument but by the oviform vases imported from China, which were then much in favor. Compare the lines of this type of Oriental vase with the splat of a simple fiddle-back chair, and the source of the idea is clear indeed (*Drawing 20*). However, names once given, even in error, have a way of sticking, "fiddle-backs" they have been called from the beginning, and as such they remain.

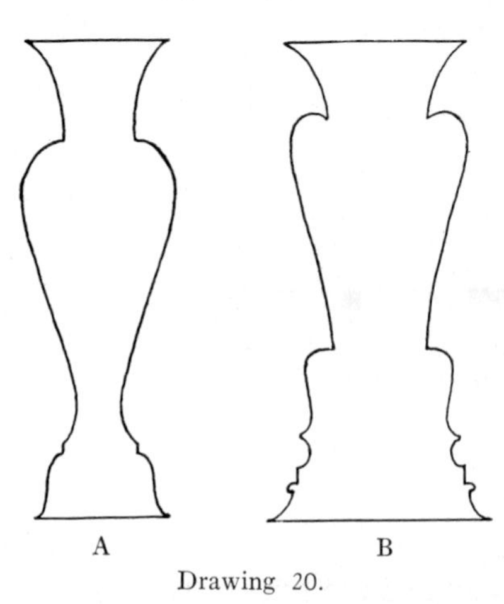

Drawing 20.

FIDDLE-BACK OUTLINES
A, simple; B, elaborate.

Except for this back piece the chairs themselves adhered in construction to that of the banister-backs and were made in two types (*Illustration 70*). The more elaborate had turned and square front legs terminating with Flemish feet; boldly turned front and side stretchers, and back uprights more or less square and shaped to conform to the back by a slight backward curve above the seat level. The front surfaces of

A B C

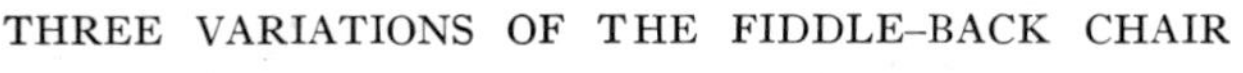

Illustration 70. THREE VARIATIONS OF THE FIDDLE–BACK CHAIR

A, Rural type of southern New England with simple turned uprights and stretchers. B, More elaborate with square back uprights, Spanish feet and back-conforming splat. C, Final form with shaped seat, cabriole legs, and flat bowed stretchers, from Rhode Island. All made *ca.* 1715–1730.

the back uprights were generally relieved by a rounding effect applied with a molding plane with narrow cockle-beading at the outer edges. The lower cross-member of the back was plain and straight, while that at the top was curved and carved in modified yoke-shape. The vase-shaped back-splat was plain and unadorned save that it too had the back-conforming bend. In the simpler types, both front and back uprights were turned in elaborate vase-shapings, the underbody stretchers plain rounds, and the upper cross-member just scroll-saw-cut into ox-yoke lines. The splat, which was more often boldly vase-shaped, was always minus the backward curve. Like the banister-back, these chairs were made with and without arms, and the seats were rush or, in the simpler ones, sometimes woven splint. Made in the native hard woods, some had splats of curly, bird's-eye maple or other fancy grained wood. With a few the yoke was fashioned of such materials. Such parts were probably varnished while the rest of the chair was painted, and in rare cases had the ring or cuff elements touched with gilt. This chair design originated about 1715, but for some unknown reason it was not adopted by craftsmen working elsewhere than in that part of New England bordering on Long Island Sound and the Atlantic to the eastward. It functioned, however, as the van for the oncoming army of Queen Anne chairs with cabriole front legs, vase-shaped splat, and tall conforming back surmounted by a carved yoke-shaped top.

These Queen Anne forms were the outcome of the bandy-legged chair introduced into England from Holland during the William and Mary period, which was ignored by American workmen save for those working in New York. The first chairs of Queen Anne influence made here had the front cabriole legs ending in pad or Dutch feet similar in shaping and curve to those used for chests of drawers and tables (*Illustration 70C*). At the knee, where the legs joined the seat frame, a bracket block was used for finish and strength. It carried the curve of the leg over to the scallop of the under edge of the frame, which flared keystone-like from the back. There was no stretcher between the front legs, but a central one connected those of each side and functioned for it. Also, between the square back legs, a little higher than those at the side, was another stretcher. All four were turned in the fundamental vase-shape. The splat of the back was plain except for its oriental-vase shaping and conforming curve, and the uprights beside it were also unadorned. Since there was no lower cross-member in the back, the base of the splat was mortised into the back element of the seat level and held at the top by a yoke-shaped cross-member with its upper side curved backward and sometimes emphasized with carved moldings of the cockle-bead type. Where the simple fiddle-backs of southern New England had seats of rush or splint, with these finer chairs the upholstered slip type was the rule.

Such chairs were made throughout New England and as far south as Delaware. Maple, walnut, and occasionally mahogany were the woods used. From the examples extant it is evident that sets of a half-dozen, with now and then an upholstered wing chair added, were not uncommon. Several sets of one wing and six side chairs, held to have been made by Job and Christopher Townsend, have been located in the past few years. In design, the wing chair has cabriole front legs and canted square rear ones which conform to those of the side chairs. These and the stretchers, however, are the only woodwork not covered by upholstery material. Seat, apron, arms, and back are entirely upholstered (*Illustration 71*). The back itself terminates in an arching curve, while the arms and wings which flare outward from the back are treated as single members with continuous lines, in contrast to the succeeding Chippendale type in which the ear-like wings and arms below were so executed that while being one piece, an impression of separation was effected.

Among the colonial shipping records of the period (1720 to 1740) still preserved in London there are a number of manifests which throw an interesting light on where these chairs were made and on the coastal trade in them. These documents

(Gallery of Fine Arts, Yale Univ.) *(Gallery of Fine Arts, Yale Univ.)*

A B

Illustration 71. THE WING CHAIR

A, Queen Anne type, *ca.* 1720–30. B, Chippendale type, *ca.* 1760–70.

record sufficient shipments of walnut lumber north from Virginia and in return walnut chairs destined for Maryland, Virginia, and Carolina ports to make it obvious that the northern cabinetmakers were even as early as this reaching out for new markets. It would be most interesting if letters or other documents could be discovered that would give more detailed information. Whether southern planters shipped their walnut North with specific orders to convert it into chairs to be returned to them, or this lumber was just a commodity that they marketed where they could and the same held true of the finished chairs, is a fine point yet to be settled. This much is clear: The fact that fiddle-backs found in the South are of southern red walnut is no proof that they were made where the wood grew. If the workmanship is either New England or Pennsylvanian in detail and feeling, it is safe to infer that they were made North and were the product of this coastal trade exchange.

Toward the close of the Queen Anne period, chairs became more elaborate. The knees of the front legs and the centre of the upper crosspiece of the back were ornamented with raised, carved shells akin to those used on the block-front chests of drawers and secretaries of the Chippendale era, and as such are harbingers of the coming of that style. Where these were used, the outline of the back-splat was made more elaborate by the addition of handle-like volutes at the widest point. Similarly some armchairs were made with skirt, arms, and supports executed in cabinet wood and varnished instead of being textile-covered. In such cases, the shaping of these parts was in relation to the curves of the cabriole legs, and the arms terminated in carved knuckles much like those then being used with Windsor chairs. All this saw further development during the Chippendale years, so that chairs of a distinct Queen Anne flavor with upholstered back and seat but wooden arms are also examples of the transition.

In fact, the shift in chair-making styles was so gradual and was marked by such small changes of construction and ornamentation that one cannot state to a year just when American craftsmen no longer incorporated Queen Anne details or lines. There seems to have been fifteen or twenty years during which chairs had about them something of both styles. The cabriole leg with pad-foot gave place to one with the claw-and-ball termination. The solid vase-shaped splat became a little more complicated in outline, and the back-conforming curve was eliminated. Then it was changed in outline to what is known as the beaker shape and pierced by scroll-saw cuttings that gave it an interlacing pattern. The scalloped apron was replaced by one straight on its under edge. The practice of rounding the corners of the front of the seat was dropped, and those almost square were restored to general use. The seats themselves became more nearly square with the outward flare from the back slightly less pronounced. The upper cross-member of the back was modified from the ox-yoke shaping to a conventionalized adaptation of the cupid's bow (*Drawing 21*). The arrangement of cross-stretches which so admirably braced the legs in the former period now disappeared. In this last detail, Philadelphians were some years ahead of the workmen of New England, who clung to this practical structural device for some time after all other traces of the earlier style had disappeared.

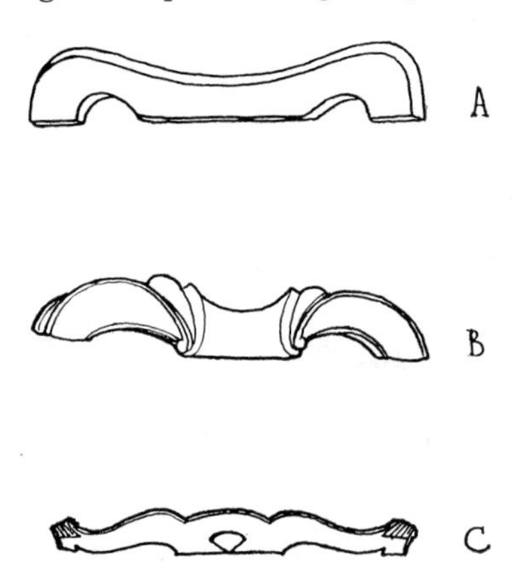

Drawing 21.

TOP CROSS-RAILS FROM QUEEN ANNE AND CHIPPENDALE CHAIR-BACKS

A, simple Queen Anne yoke; B, yoke elaborated with carving; C, cupid's bow form of the Chippendale.

And now, like an individual sloughing off all marks of a former existence, the Queen Anne fiddle-back emerged as the typical Chippendale with cabriole leg, claw-and-ball foot, and interlaced openwork back-splat. Such chairs were, of course,

A

(*Gallery of Fine Arts, Yale Univ.*)

B

(*Gallery of Fine Arts, Yale Univ.*)

C

Illustration 72. CHIPPENDALE CHAIRS

A, Chair with cabriole legs, claw-and-ball feet, and intricately cut back splat. Made in New England between 1760 and 1770. B, Roundabout chair with carved ornamentation. C, Gothic Chippendale with square legs. Details of the back indicate Philadelphia origin. Made 1760–1775.

made of mahogany, and some of them had much fine carving at the knees of the front legs, across the top of the back, and on the front surface of the back-splat. Surviving examples indicate that the craftsmen of Philadelphia as a group produced finer and more elaborate chairs of this type than did those of the other colonies. On their best pieces they lavished a wealth of carving so fine that casual inspection might almost lead one to pronounce them of English make. The sample chairs of Benjamin Randolph referred to in Part One show the "height of elegance" some of our native craftsmen could attain if they could find customers willing to foot the bill. Indeed, the decade from 1760 to 1770 may be said to mark the zenith of superior chair-making in America (*Illustration 16A*).

But this was not the only design of chair in the Chippendale manner. A few were made in which the claw-and-ball foot, acanthus-leaf carving at front knees, and other details were replaced by oriental fretwork which was the American adaptation of the Chinese Chippendale. Again, if the piercings of the splat were Gothic in curve, the chair was of course an example of Gothic Chippendale. Then there were roundabouts with a single or three cabriole legs ending in claw-and-ball feet supporting the diagonally placed square seat. The upper ends of three of these legs supported a low rounded backpiece akin to those used with the low-backed Windsors. Between back and seat level on two sides were pierced splats. Such chairs were of course designed for a corner, and had been made in England for a long time, but were more or less of a novelty here (*Illustration 72*).

To match the tables with severely plain square legs devoid of curve or taper, chairs with legs of the same order were made. In them the underbody was provided with four stretchers, one on each side connected by a cross-stretcher set back three or four inches from the front legs and the fourth, between the back legs, located a little higher than those at the sides. Some of these chairs had a back design approximating that of the cabriole-leg type, but more of them were of the ladder-back

Illustration 73. *(Gallery of Fine Arts, Yale Univ.)*

A CHIPPENDALE CHAIR WITH LADDER BACK

Chairs of this type are probably rarer than other Chippendale styles. The one shown is of Philadelphia or Baltimore origin between 1760 and 1770.

style (*Illustration 73*). This term designates the chair in which the vertical splat was replaced by three horizontal members conforming in curve to that of the top rail. Because of its similarity to a section of ladder, the name has attached itself to chairs of this type. The cross-members (including that at the top) usually were pierced and sometimes had a slightly carved boss at the centre of each. Ladder-backs, as well as those with the ornamental splat-back, were generally made in sets. Two arm and six side chairs were standard. Where arms were attached, they flared outward from the back with curves of the cyma order and were supported at the front by uprights set three or four inches behind the front legs. These were curved in outline, and the front ends of the arms always ended in carved knuckles which curved both outward and downward, as did those of the banister-back chairs. With both splat- and ladder-back styles the slip-seat was the usual treatment. Occasionally with some of the latter the textile of the seat was brought over and covered the members connecting the legs at seat level.

When upholstered chairs were made with squared legs, the back was generally high with a simple arched curve, and the arms simple downward curves from the back ending squarely without knuckle carving. The Benjamin Franklin chair now owned by Columbia University is typical. In the wing chair, either cabriole legs with claw feet or plain square ones were used (*Illustration 71*). Both these and the arm chairs with upholstered backs were made in two sizes: the larger for the master, and another about a quarter smaller in all dimensions for the mistress of the house. Here we have the first evidence of a distinct move toward giving women some ease in sitting. Martha Washington is known to have had such a chair at Mount Vernon. Now all American Chippendale easy-chairs of the three-quarters size are consistently dubbed Martha Washingtons. (*Illustration 74.*)

It is difficult to state with finality just what upholstery materials were used originally for chair coverings. There were morocco leather, various kinds of damask, and, most emphatically, haircloth, that long-wearing material which so endeared itself to thrifty Americans. It continued in popularity for a century or more. In 1765 there is a reference to this material in a

Illustration 74. *(Gallery of Fine Arts, Yale Univ.)*

HEPPLEWHITE ARMCHAIR WITH UPHOLSTERED BACK

Chairs of this type of smaller size are called Martha Washington chairs. *Ca.* 1790.

letter written by Mrs. Benjamin Franklin to her husband, then in London as agent for the American Colonies. "The chairs are plain horsehair," she wrote, "and look as well as Paduasoy." The latter material was a special silken upholstery fabric originating at Padua, the Italian city long known for its excellent textiles. What capital an enterprising manufacturer would make of such an endorsement today! In a full-page advertisement with appropriate pictures and signature he would set forth: "Mrs. Benjamin Franklin uses haircloth. Distinguished Philadelphia matron and wife of our commissioner at English Court considers it proper for her drawing-room chairs."

Among the known cabinetmakers, whose chairs done in the Chippendale manner are either labeled or of such distinctive work as to make it possible to ascribe specific pieces to them, we have William Savery, James Gillingham, Benjamin Randolph, and Jonathan Gostelowe, all of Philadelphia. These men ornamented their chairs with carving on a par at times with those from the master's own shop and, in those early days, possibly from his own hands. (*Illustration 16.*)

By some curious coincidence there are no Chippendale chairs bearing the imprint of the work of the Townsend-Goddards of Rhode Island. Fine and distinctive as were their secretaries, chests of drawers, and tables, their chairs were not fashioned with enough individuality to distinguish them from others of New England origin.

In New York, where outstanding cabinetmakers did not flourish until well after the Chippendale period, there was one exception. A single chair bearing the label of Gilbert Ash proves that his work was fine enough to be easily mistaken for that of the Philadelphia group. Yet the market for fine chairs in New York must have been meager indeed. The records show that in 1765, although he had a shop on Wall Street, the poor artist was forced to follow two trades in order to eke out an existence. One was that of chair-maker and the other the noisome calling of soap-boiler! Whether Thomas Ash and

Thomas Ash, Jr., outstanding chair-makers in the early 19th Century, were his descendants is not clear. If so, they had moved up the social scale a number of notches, for they held several posts of distinction and were affluent enough to sit to Sully and other portrait painters. Identifying Gilbert Ash further and proving his relationship to the two Thomases, father and son, is an assignment awaiting somebody that might throw much needed light on the cabinetmakers of New York before the days of Phyfe.

The American Chippendale chairs seem all to have been produced in the twenty years ending with 1770. Then came fifteen unsettled years. The American Revolution was brewing and being fought to a conclusion. The progress of the British expeditionary forces from Boston to Yorktown with side excursions to Saratoga, coastal South Carolina, and elsewhere, together with a Continental paper currency printed with reckless disregard of the lack of bullion, were not conducive to fine chair-making. Naturally during these years people either made shift to use what they had or, if new chairs were imperative, turned to the less expensive Windsors and slat-backs.

But once peace was established, the decade and a half suspension in making chairs of the better grades afforded craftsmen a wide-open market. And now, as with other pieces of furniture, they worked in a new style. Where formerly, in spite of grace of line and beauty of ornamentation, chairs had been ponderous, those done in the Hepplewhite had a lightsomeness approaching that of a graceful woman in her early twenties (*Illustration 75*).

While in other pieces the Hepplewhite style was basically straight of line, the chairs combined straight lines for the underbody with delightful curves for the outline of the back. The legs were tapered and sometimes ended with spade-feet. Also the front legs were occasionally ornamented with reeding that gave them something of the fluted square column or pilaster effect. If there were stretchers—more often there were

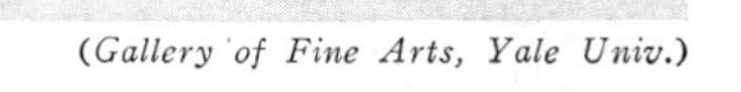

(*Gallery of Fine Arts, Yale Univ.*)

A B C

Illustration 75.

HEPPLEWHITE CHAIRS

A, Sidechair with cross stretchers and carving on legs. B, Sidechair with all ornamentation on shield-shaped back. C, Armchair with plainer treatment of back and without spade feet. All three made between 1785 and 1800.

not—they were plain rectangular members of light proportions.

From this classically simple frame there sprouted a shield-shaped back with arched crosspiece at the top and a deep U-shaped curve continuous from upper corner to upper corner but connected to the back legs by curving offsets. This might have four or five verticals that branched out from the bottom of the shield and curved slightly upward, or they could be more elaborate. Again, the shield-shape was sometimes modified by intertwining volutes so that the effect was that of an oval superimposed on the shield. Reeding, carving, and generally a small sunburst inlay at the lower point of the shield were all used as ornamentation. Although the backs were formed with curved lines, the latter were so skillfully employed that they served to accentuate rather than contradict the straightness of the legs.

Samuel McIntire, the Salem carver and cabinetmaker, and Duncan Phyfe of New York both produced some very fine examples of chairs done in the Hepplewhite manner, as did many unknown workmen of New England and Pennsylvania. When chairs of this style were made with arms, they were much like those used in the Chippendale chairs of the Martha Washington type. Mahogany was the wood chiefly used, but occasionally excellent examples were made by country cabinetmakers in cherry.

The seats were always upholstered; and the usual, if not the invariable, practice was to cover the seat frame, which flared outward from the back and often had a curved front, with the textile so that the only wood visible was that of the legs and back. Large brass-headed tacks, either plain or in festoon patterns, were used to give finish to the edges of the upholstery. From 1780 to 1800 can properly be considered the Hepplewhite years in chair-making, and probably the majority were produced in the decade from 1785 to 1795.

With the advent of the 19th Century, American craftsmen put aside the style of George Hepplewhite for that of Thomas Sheraton, the Englishman who combined the calling

Illustration 76. SHERATON CHAIR STYLES

A, With upright back splats. B, With urn-shaped central splat and frame. C, With cross bars. *Ca.* 1815–1825.

of furniture designer with the avocation of preacher and author of religious tracts—to the probable detriment of the former, since the latter kept him continually "out of funds." Instead of the shield-backs they now made one with a horizontal top cross-member and three or four vertical uprights which generally widened as they joined the upper crosspiece; and the front was carved in conventionalized leaf patterns (*Illustration* 76). I think that, although Sheraton never left England, the palm tree was his inspiration for this effect. At times these upright slats were combined with carved draperies alone or with an urn-shaping. This combination was not employed in many American chairs. The square, tapered legs of the previous period now became turned and reeded like those of tables and other pieces of the Sheraton influence, only of more delicate proportions. Chair seats were either approximately square, flaring slightly forward from the back, or curved in a ball-like silhouette.

When the French Directoire reached America (as translated into Anglo-Saxon by Sheraton for the better understanding of both our cabinetmakers and their customers), the chair-back resulted in which a nicely formed lyre made of a combination of mahogany and brass rods to simulate the strings of that musical instrument and set between horizontal upper and lower cross-members. With this, the framework of the chair harked back to the Roman curule form that has a slightly concave back and simple, chaste lines for both front and back legs. As made by the Americans, these legs were square of cross-section and were given graceful but balancing curves. The outer surface, particularly of the front legs and the back ones above the seat level, was usually ornamented with parallel lines of reeding. Sometimes the front legs might even have this surface covered with an all-over acanthus-leaf design. A few done by Phyfe had paw feet and carving to simulate fur halfway up the front legs. In fact, this New York cabinetmaker made so many fine examples of the lyre-back chair that all of them are now called Phyfe regardless of

(*Metropolitan Museum of Art*)

A

(*Gallery of Fine Arts, Yale Univ.*)

B

(*Metropolitan Museum of Art*)

C

Illustration 77.

TYPICAL PHYFE CHAIRS

A, His lyre-back chair. B, Chair with curved back members. C, Simpler chair with single horizontal back splat. All three were made in his best manner and before 1825.

whether the details are as finely executed as was the standard for his shops (*Illustration 77*).

Another variety of the American Sheraton was the chair with tapered, reeded front legs and openwork back in which a single cross-slat with cyma curves was set. This back had a lower horizontal crossbar, and above it a pair of diagonal slats forming an X either straight or elliptically curved. Mahogany was the wood used for these fine chairs, and most of them were equipped with slip-seats although some, such as the bell-seat, had the material tacked directly to the chair-frame. With none save occasional armchairs were stretchers used.

Contemporary with these types, American chair-makers developed the painted fancy chair which was made of maple or possibly a softer wood and, when finished, painted and gilded. In some the turnings were given slight double rings to simulate bamboo, and the backs were formed both by vertical and by horizontal turnings or splats. This chair form was produced in large quantities by Hitchcock and hundreds of other chair-makers during our Empire years (*Illustration 78*). It usually had six cross-stretchers, two at each side and one at front and back. With the earliest, the seat may have been woven cane, but it shortly gave way to rush and was only revived in the last years of the Empire style.

The Boston rocker, that universal favorite of American women from 1820 to the Civil War days, was a hybrid. It had elements of the painted fancy, the decadent Windsor and the 17th Century rod-back. The identity of its inventor is still shrouded in mystery, but the name indicates birth in the town of beans and brown bread. (*Illustration 79.*) Structurally the seat, underbody, and arms were decadent Windsor; the upper crosspiece of the back was painted fancy, and the spindles, usually seven in number, were reminiscent of the much earlier rod-back. In finish, the stenciling and gilding superimposed on the dark background were painted fancy while the grained seat and pencil-stripings of back spindles and turned members of the underbody were the usual trappings

Illustration 78. *(Metropolitan Museum of Art)*

A PAINTED FANCY CHAIR

Made about 1815, it is typical of the thousands that were produced by chair makers in America for about a quarter of a century.

Illustration 79.

A BOSTON ROCKER

This chair form was a descendant of the Windsor rocking chair and was made widely from 1820 until 1850. The one shown dates from about 1830 and represents the Boston rocker at its best.

of the low-back decadent Windsors. In some of the late examples of these rockers, the solid wooden seat with its front roll and upward back-curve was cut away for a central panel of cane. Hitchcock and other fancy chair-makers produced Boston rockers in quantity. There are records showing that from about 1835 to 1850, Cincinnati, Ohio, boasted a "Boston Rocker Manufactory" that was kept busy supplying the women of the Ohio and Mississippi Valleys with this comfortable and inexpensive chair in which they could "set and rock."

When by 1820 the American Empire vogue began to replace the Regency mode of Sheraton (from which in truth it sprang), much of the furniture was gross and graceless, as has been bluntly pointed out in earlier chapters. Chairs, however, were the exception. The mahogany, or sometimes maple, sidechair which these years brought forth, with its solid lyre-shaped back-splat, arched top, and general lines like the old Roman curule, was neat and artistic (*Illustration 80*). It lacked the reeding of the Sheraton chair of the same general lines and fortunately was severely simple. First-quality mahogany was used throughout, and the face of the back-splat and the upper crosspiece was covered with well-marked crotch veneer, which was ornament enough. Happily, many thousand sets of this design were produced before our chair-makers were bitten by the fatal bug of self-expression. Then in their struggle for originality they made changes in the lyre outline, complicated it, added carving, substituted turned spindles for the single splat and ran amuck generally. So passed this perfectly good design, and the result was Empire stuff.

From the Queen Anne through the Hepplewhite years the more elaborate chairs were also produced by American workmen in double- or love-seat forms (*Illustration 81A*). In essence they simply brought two armchairs together and, omitting the central pairs of arms and one pair of front and rear legs, made in line a single piece of furniture that was, so to speak, a Siamese twin. In rural sections during the 18th and early 19th Century, double chairs were frequently made of the

Illustration 80.

AN AMERICAN EMPIRE CHAIR OF MAPLE WITH TURNED LEGS

From 1825 simple chairs of this design were made for two decades in many chair shops throughout New England.

A

Illustration 81. B

CITY AND COUNTRY LOVE SEATS OR DOUBLE CHAIRS

A, Chippendale type from Philadelphia. *Ca.* 1760. B, Farm wagon seat of about 1820.

Illustration 82.

PAINTED FANCY SETTEE OF HITCHCOCK TYPE

Such benches were made and decorated as shown from 1815 to 1830. The design of the stencil indicates Pennsylvania origin.

slat-back variety. The chief use for them with their six legs, parallel tiers of cross-slats, and rush or splint seats was to convert the general utility farm wagon into a conveyance for the family. Hence these slat-back love seats are commonly known as wagon seats. (*Illustration 81B.*)

In my own family, there is a tradition that on Sunday mornings a great-grandfather swept clean the box of his farm wagon, lined it with fresh straw, and into it set three wagon seats. Then he was ready for church. The homely cart thus had a seating capacity equal to his family of three boys and five girls and great-grandsire could drive with dignity and Spartan simplicity to the New England meetinghouse some miles away. We regret that after the Civil War this set of wagon seats was considered too crude for anything but kindling wood. Had they been preserved, they would now be most convenient, indoors and out, examples.

With the painted fancy chair, the trend was to produce it in triple or quadruple form rather than double. So instead of love seats, benches accommodating four, six, or even eight people were made. Some had rush or cane seats but the majority had stout wooden seats fashioned from a single piece of pine like those used with Windsor settees. Some were made with ornamentally turned spindles for back and arms, an upper horizontal backpiece extending the entire length that was shaped by scroll sawing, and nicely curved arms (*Illustration 82*). Such benches usually had eight legs and neatly proportioned cross-stretchers, simply turned. When so made, they were an attempt to approximate, in bench form, a piece of furniture nearly as ornamental as the sofa then so popular for parlor use or disuse. The painting and gilding was elaborate and was done in a number of colors. Then there were benches where no effort at ornamental refinements was attempted. They were intended for court rooms, church parlors, and schools, and so were the unadorned, hard-working members of the furniture family. They are interesting as a type but not particularly desirable from the collector's viewpoint.

CHAPTER SIX

WINDSOR CHAIRS

THE Windsor chair, like many other things American, was an immigrant. Originating in England, it crossed the Atlantic and prospered beyond all expectation. American craftsmen seized on the idea and converted it from a simple piece of cottage furniture to one on which they could expend an infinite amount of artistic skill.

For many years the story of the discovery of this chair by George III in a farm cottage near Windsor Castle has been conceded to be the correct version of its origin. It undoubtedly took its name from the town where it first came to popular notice, but at St. Cross Hospital, Winchester, England, there is a Gothic chair of the 13th Century which is the Windsor in its earliest form (*Illustration 83*).

This ancestor with its low back proves that the type of chair known as Windsor was in existence some centuries before George III dropped into a cottage of a rainy afternoon and found it a comfortable and attractive part of the furnishings. The close relationship between the 13th Century chair and Windsors as we know them is further substantiated by the fact that the decadent forms made in the United States as late as 1880 follow very closely the lines of their Gothic ancestor. Many of us can well remember the heavy, wooden-seated chairs with low U-back and spindles that were so common in fire houses, country hotels, general stores, and other public places. Made of pine and painted, they invited jackknife carving and were often liberally decorated with initials.

Windsors seem to have made their appearance in America

about 1700. First settling in the City of Brotherly Love, they were called Philadelphia chairs. From there they migrated up and down the Atlantic seaboard, and various localities developed distinct types. Thus we have the Connecticut Windsor with turnings of leg and spindles and general proportions quite different from those of Rhode Island, Massachusetts, New York, and Pennsylvania.

Illustration 83.

THE GOTHIC ANCESTOR OF THE WINDSOR CHAIR

This chair is large and strong enough to seat a knight in full armor.

As this sort of chair-making spread, it developed structurally, taking on ornamental high-backs with single or double combs, as well as the simple hoop-back with or without arms. Likewise there appeared the Windsor settle, which was often a most graceful piece of furniture, and the Windsor writing-chair. The latter, with its broad arm, was the grandfather of the one-arm lunch chair.

Not a few Windsors were present at important American historical events. When the first Continental Congress met in Carpenter's Hall, Philadelphia, to think about revolting from the English king, its members sat in Windsor chairs which are still to be seen in that historic building. The presiding officer used an elaborate and graceful Windsor typical of the best workmanship of Philadelphia chair-makers.

Richmonde, first name unknown, of Sassafras Street, Philadelphia, seems to be the first identified American craftsman who devoted himself to Windsor chair-making, and the similarity between an identified chair of his make and these historic ones in Carpenter's Hall makes it seem probable that they, too, came from his shop.

The next year, when the Continental Congress came together

Illustration 84. *(American Philosophical Society)*

THE CRADLE OF THE DECLARATION OF INDEPENDENCE

Thomas Jefferson's writing Windsor. Seated in it, he wrote the first draft of that important document. Made about 1760 with reconstructions that may date as late as 1810.

at Independence Hall to adopt the Declaration, it was from Windsor chairs that the members rose to sign that momentous document. Not far from this spot, in the collection of the American Philosophical Society, there is another Windsor which also played a part in making the Declaration of Independence an accomplished fact. This chair with wide writing-arm once belonged to Thomas Jefferson (*Illustration 84*). Seated in it, he penned the first draft of that famous document which begins, "When, in the course of human events . . ."

Jefferson, in addition to being a great statesman and consummate politician, was an architect and engineer of ability. His chair has a number of unique features. It revolves as do our present-day office chairs. Also the writing-arm is pivoted so that the sitter may draw it close to him as he writes.

Windsors also played their part in the private life of George and Martha Washington. After the Revolution, when Washington returned to Mount Vernon, there was such a constant stream of visitors that, to accommodate them, thirty Windsors were ordered for the east portico. Seated in these, the visitors waited their audience with the retired Commander-in-Chief. Mrs. Washington chose to have them sit on these sturdy chairs rather than rack the delicate mahogany Hepplewhites in her drawing room.

This purchase of Windsors by the Washingtons is particularly interesting in light of the fact that before the difference with England, Washington, in ordering chairs from his London agent, complained that those natively made were "not strong enough for common sitting." Either our chair-makers had improved their product, or Washington's patriotism led him to overlook the frailty of domestic workmanship.

In Connecticut, Windsors also were present on the governmental scene. When the old statehouse at Hartford was built, John Wadsworth provided Windsor chairs and settees to furnish it. For these he was paid 70 pounds, 13 shillings. A newspaper advertisement by Wadsworth in the *American Mercury* of January 4, 1796, states that he has come "to Hartford to carry on the Windsor chairmaking business," and that he would like "one or two likely boys, 13 or 14 years old," as apprentices and would "purchase a quantity of square edged white planks, from 18 to 20 inches wide." This lumber he evidently needed for Windsor chair-seats, since pine or white wood was the favorite material.

In New York City, Andrew Gautier was the first Windsor chair-maker of record. Born there in 1720 of Huguenot parentage, he early established himself as a Windsor chair-maker. He was a liberal user of newspaper advertising, and probably the first to illustrate his advertisement. In the *New York Gazette* of April 18, 1765, appeared one of his illustrated advertisements, which read in part:

> A large and neat assortment of Windsor Chairs, made in the best and neatest manner, and well painted: Such as, high backed, low backed, and saddle backed chairs and settees; fit for piazza or garden,—children's dining and low chairs.
>
> N.B.—As the above Gautier intends to keep a large number of all sorts: all persons wanting such may depend on being supplied with any quantity,—wholesale or retail—at reasonable rates.

The illustration shows a typical Philadelphia Windsor with high comb-back; but the drawing is so bad that the chair seems to be falling apart. Evidently newspaper readers of 1765 did not require the accuracy of pictorial appeal that rules today.

Among other New York Windsor craftsmen were McBride; John K. Cowperthwaite, who founded the furniture business that still bears his name; Thomas Ash, and his son, Thomas, Jr. The elder Ash, with his shop at 33 John Street, was a man of importance and of many affairs. For years he was treasurer of the Tammany Society. It was in his shop that Robert Tweed, father of the famous Boss Tweed, learned the chair-making trade which the boss also followed until he retired to devote himself to politics and the upbuilding of the notorious Ring.

In addition to the few Windsor chair-makers mentioned, there was hardly a sizable village which did not have its own maker of these chairs. I believe, if an accurate list could be compiled, the total number would easily pass the half-thousand mark and would include men working all the way from Maine to the Carolinas.

American Windsors can readily be distinguished from those

A B

Illustration 85.

PHILADELPHIA WINDSORS

A, low-back; B, low-back with comb added and nine spindles lengthened. The leg turnings of both are characteristic of Philadelphia work, as are the shaping of the seats and the back structure. *Ca.* 1750–1770.

of England by two earmarks. The English chairs have an ornamental splat that replaces the center spindles of the back, and there is decidedly less splay, or slope, to the legs. In variety of form and structural detail American Windsors show clearly the evolutionary forces that affected them. Starting with a form closely akin to the Gothic prototype, this type of chair was produced by American craftsmen for a century and a quarter, during which we see it grow up and, in its old age, veer around to a debased interpretation of the original. This senile decay produced the heavy low-backed chair that marked the end of the Windsor years and is not of itself worth collecting except to show how low this style fell.

Philadelphia was the first place of record where American Windsors were made. From here the craft spread northward, and the extensive coastal trade made the use of Windsors general in the South. Practically no chairs of this type in the southern Atlantic area were locally produced. When one is found of proven southern birth, its lines and details show that it was made by a northern artisan who had migrated.

The earliest Philadelphia Windsors were of the low-back design with a heavy U-shaped top rail and a deep, well-molded seat conforming in outline to the upper rail (*Illustration 85A*). Generally from ten to twelve plain spindles, about half an inch in diameter and slightly tapering, formed the back. At the front, two heavier, ornamentally turned spindles provided the uprights to support the rails, which sometimes had a centre-cresting and an outward curve at the extremes. The legs were well splayed, and in turning were of the so-called blunt-arrow design terminating in a ball-like foot. The stretchers connecting the front and rear legs were simple in outline and marked with a bulbous turning in the centre. The cross-stretcher, on the other hand, was often elaborately turned and provided a major item of ornamentation. Well executed ball-and-ring turnings are characteristic of this centre brace.

Since chairs of this early type were essentially for men, they were of ample proportions and sturdily built. They were good sensible pieces of furniture in which hearty males of six feet and two hundred pounds could loll without fear of the casualties liable to frailer pieces. But the back was only ten or twelve inches above the seat and left something to be desired in comfort; so the first step in the development of the Windsor came about.

This was the comb-back (*Illustration 85B*). Here, with details of seat, legs, stretchers, and top rail unchanged, seven or nine of the back spindles were extended upward for about eighteen inches and surmounted by a cross-member in outline much like the upper edge of the ornamental comb then worn by women. While the upper rail in the earliest types of the comb-back remained unchanged, craftsmen soon realized that this member no longer needed to be so sturdy; and so they began to make it lighter and lighter. It lost its cresting and became uniform in thickness. Ornamentation was transferred to the comb, which developed slightly carved ends called ears.

Drawing 22.

A FAN–BACK WINDSOR WITH ARMS

From the comb-back chair emerged the fan-back (*Drawing 22*). Here the seat, legs, and stretchers remained the same; but the back underwent further modification. The comb was enlarged and made stouter. The old upper rail disappeared and was replaced by arms extending forward from the outer spindles of the back, which, since they were now exterior members, were made heavier and were more elaborately turned. With the omission of arms the fan-back side chair appeared and marked the end of the Windsor as a purely male piece of furniture.

While the comb- and fan-back types were being evolved, the bow-back was also coming into being. It, too, was based on the Philadelphia low-back chair, and was an answer to the problem of making the Windsor more comfortable by increasing its back. Here the upper ends of the lengthened spindles were made fast in a round hoop that extended in an arc from just behind the second spindle. This hoop, always somewhat heavier than the spindles, was never ornamented for the excellent reason that it was impossible to fashion it so that it could be bent in the necessary arc and at the same time elaborate it with turnings (*Drawing 23*).

In time the fan-back exerted its influence on this type and bow-backs were made in which the upper rail of the original chair disappeared. By skillful shaping and bending, the hoop was made to extend continuously from front spindle to front spindle in an unbroken line with no support for the spindles of the back at the point where the upper rail of the low-back existed (*Illustration 86*). Thus the one-piece bow-back style developed. Here, too, the bow-back sometimes lost its arms and became a simple side chair of more ladylike proportions (*Drawing 24*). Similarly, combs were added by extending some of the spindles through the hoop and terminating them several inches above with a comb-piece. This provided a chair with a high back and above that a most convenient head rest.

Drawing 23.

A BOW-BACK WINDSOR WITH COMB PIECE

As these different types evolved, American ingenuity added one more improvement. The back with spindles held in place by various sorts of outer frames was the weakest part. Heavy people tilting backward put too great a strain on it. To correct this, braces were introduced. These extended from the points of the hoop downward in a V to a projection of the seat of three to six inches called the tailpiece. These braces added

Illustration 86. *(Metropolitan Museum of Art)*

A NEW ENGLAND WINDSOR

The one-piece back, braces, and comb are not often found in combination. Made about 1760–1775.

strength and lines which made for a new beauty of detail (*Illustration 87*).

Windsors were also affected by the stylistic trend of the Sheraton period. Then it was that the chair appeared with a back made entirely of turned spindles of approximately the same diameter and without ring-and-ball turnings. This was the rod-back chair and was a combination of the Windsor idea and Sheraton simplicity (*Drawing 25*).

Drawing 24.

A HOOP-BACK WINDSOR

This type was not often made with arms.

The writing chair evolved in the period when the Windsor was essentially masculine. Here the makers hit on the sensible idea of enlarging one arm and making a combination chair and desk. As most people are right-handed, the majority of Windsor writing chairs have the small table-top attached to the dexter side; but sometimes one is found where the tablet is on the left, proving that south-paws occur in any age. At first this writing-arm was simply a little shelf affixed to the arm by a bolt or pin and so arranged that it could be swung into the desired position when in use. From that rudimentary fabrication the writing-arm underwent elaboration and became firmly fixed in the desired position with two or three spindles extending from seat to arm. Also one or more drawers for paper, quill pens, ink horns, and sand sifters for blotting were added.

Although the style details of American Windsors went through a cycle during the century of their heyday, the way they were made and wood used changed little. Soon after these chairs came into popular favor certain cabinetmakers

Illustration 87.

A HOOP–BACK WINDSOR WITH BRACES

Made in western Connecticut between 1770 and 1785.

forsook general work and, as Windsor chair-makers, devoted themselves to this piece of furniture and its variations. This, I believe, explains the skill of execution which so many of these chairs bespeak, and the numberless minor differences in design. It is obvious that, if a good craftsman limits himself to just one piece of furniture, he will evolve variations both of structure and of ornamentation that make for individuality. "Made in the neatest manner and according to the latest designs," was the phrase used in many of the advertisements of the early Windsor makers.

Drawing 25.

A ROD-BACK WINDSOR

It was made with and without arms.

In making these chairs even the few power tools then available were little used. While the deep turnings of the underbody parts were always the result of skillful use of lathe and turning chisels (as were also the exterior spindles), the delicate uprights of the rest of the back and the round piece that formed the hoop of the chair when it was a bow-back were not lathe-produced. These slightly tapering spindles were fashioned with draw- and spoke-shaves guided by a keen eye. If you have ever tried to make even so simple a thing as a walking stick from a sapling, you can appreciate the skill attained by these chair-makers. Sometimes for the decoration of the back a slight bulbous detail was added to the spindles which, if not uniform, would spoil the entire effect.

In the latter days of the Windsor, when bamboo turnings were so much in vogue, legs, stretchers, exterior spindles, and those of the back were made on a ring-lathe because to simulate the growth joints of bamboo by other methods was impossible.

For fashioning the seat, handwork guided by the eye of a skillful workman was employed. The concave shaping of the upper side was accomplished by chisels and small planes, while the chamfer of the edge of the seat was brought about with draw- and spoke-shaves. For the low backs of the early chairs it was a question of proper use of saws, chisels, and planes, but the making of hoops and combs demonstrated the true skill of a master. By steaming and bending into the desired shape these were rapidly put into place before the wood cooled and lost its pliability. Look at a one-piece bow-back or a single or double comb-back for an example of the ability of these workmen in the matter of steaming and bending curved parts.

A unique feature of Windsor chair-making was the use of green wood—lumber fresh from the log and still damp with the tree sap. Seats, legs, and stretchers were frequently so made. Here the ends of legs and stretchers were inserted in adjoining members with the upper ends of the legs going through the seat. In such assembling, if woods of proper grain were used, the shrinking that resulted from the seasoning made joints firmer and tighter than these could be made with the best of seasoned wood and first-quality glue.

Windsors were never made all of one wood but of a variety, each carefully selected for the strain it must suffer through years of none too careful use. Since originally all Windsors were painted, the use of several woods did not detract from the beauty of the piece. Pine and whitewood were the favorites for the seat. Sawing these bottoms from plank two inches thick and nearly two feet wide, and the ease of shaping and modeling the saddle-like concave upper side, plus the strength of such woods when seasoned, were the reasons for their selection. For the nicely turned legs, stretchers, and exterior spindles maple, birch, ash, or chestnut was generally used because they worked well in turning. Sometimes all-lathed parts were of the same wood. Among the Windsors which I have studied closely I have found chairs where these parts were of two or more woods and a few examples where oak had been used. In the decadent period pine and spruce turned parts made their appearance and the use of hard woods was dropped. White oak, hickory, and ash were the preferred woods for spindles, hoops, and back rails since they did not tend to fracture when steamed and bent to the desired shape.

Where there was a U-shaped upper rail it was made of white oak sawed in one piece to the desired curve. The knuckles or other ornamental finish of the ends were of course shaped with carving chisels. With the early Philadelphia low-back chairs the cresting of the upper rail was made of a separate piece of wood glued in place. This is, I believe, the only place in any but decadent Windsors where "built-up" construction was employed.

The comb, a structural detail first used with roundabout chairs antedating Windsors of this type, is of Greek origin. Its shaping and the carving of its ears are distinctly reminiscent of the Ionic column capital. When the two are compared, it is evident that the shaping and carved volutes of the comb-piece were inspired by this classic capital more directly than we realize. (*Drawing 26.*) The comb-piece of fan-back and other chairs was made either of oak or of hickory. First it was shaped flat, the scroll carving of the ears done, holes for the spindles bored, and then the desired curve accomplished by steam-bending. For chairs with the semicircular hoop, this piece was first shaped and then bent after proper steaming. Oak or hickory was used.

As stated earlier, some Windsors were put together green. The natural drying of wood that still had sap in it shrunk these to a tightness that would withstand many years of hard use. For chairs made entirely of seasoned parts, wedges and small wooden pins were used. The usual practice was to make the legs fast in the seat with wedges driven downward. It was also the accepted method for making spindles and arms fast. With stretchers, either pins or blind-wedging was the custom. Here small wedges were driven into the ends of the stretchers before they were fitted into their sockets, holes bored but halfway through. When the underbody parts were brought into proper alignment these concealed wedges were forced home and made joints of surprising tightness.

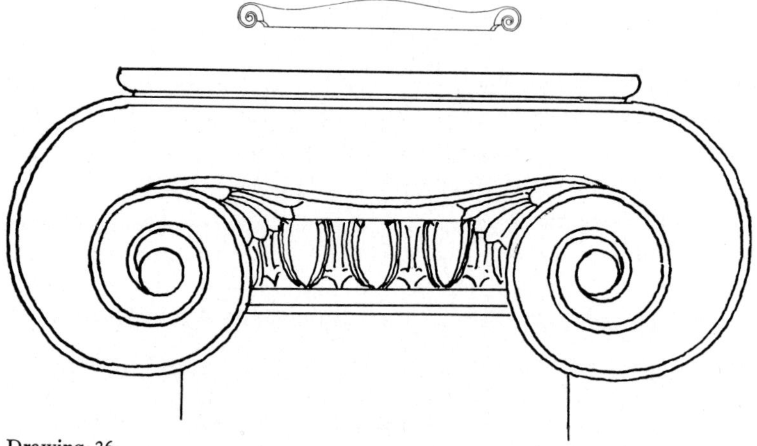

Drawing 26.

WINDSOR COMB PIECE AND IONIC COLUMN CAPITAL
Similarity of outline shows clearly the classical inspiration of the comb piece.

Sometimes hoop-back chairs are found in which blind wedges have been used at the upper ends of the spindles as well as with the stretchers. To take such chairs apart is almost impossible. There is no practical way to release the concealed wedges, and more often a broken leg, stretcher, spindle, or hoop is the result.

After joining, Windsors were smoothed with scrapers and the like. Then they were ready for painting. This was probably done by the chair-makers themselves and not by separate workers, for none of the old advertisements indicate that these chairs were sold "in the white"—in the natural wood without paint or varnish. There are plenty of references to other furniture being marketed in this condition, but not to Windsors. Instead they were given two or three coats of paint. The favorite colors were green, brown, red, and sometimes a chrome yellow.

Old newspaper advertisements show that the colors used were fairly well standardized. In Rhode Island there was a deep bottle-green that was widely advertised as Windsor chair paint. Besides the colors mentioned, black may have been used, but too few chairs with this for the original shade have been found to warrant naming it as an accepted finish of the period. For the decadent chairs, graining in reddish or brownish shades was very popular. With these, further ornamentation was accomplished by yellow stripings not unlike those with which carriages were decorated.

In approximating age, the best guide is to observe structure. Windsors of the 1725–1750 period—these dates should be considered elastically—were of the simple low-back style. After this came the comb-, fan-, and bow-back designs with and without arms. These continued to be made until the beginning of the 19th Century, when Sheraton rod-back chairs and those with bamboo turnings came into vogue. The painted "fancy" chairs also began to have an influence, and some were produced that varied noticeably from the distinct Windsor tradition.

By 1840, the clumsy fire-house chair had made its appearance, and this decadent type continued to be made until the late eighties. With the beginning of the 20th Century came a revival of the Windsor which has persisted down to the present time. Some of these latter-day chairs adhere closely to the old models. Others have hybrid adaptations such as a rush seat or the use of mahogany throughout.

A sure sign of recent make is the use of parts made of "built-up" material—several pieces of wood glued together to obtain needed dimensions. Antique Windsors always have seats fashioned from a solid piece of plank, and legs and stretchers were always turned from one-piece stock. Similarly in details of construction and shaping of leg and stretcher will be found the indications that bespeak locality of origin.

While there are exceptions, study of these points shows that there were two schools of Windsor chair-making, the Philadelphia and the New England. To the former can be ascribed those made in Pennsylvania, the Jerseys, and pre-Revolutionary New York; to the latter, the chairs made in New York after the Revolution and all of the area to the north and east. Why New York chairs should be Philadelphia in feeling before 1775 and New England afterward is hard to explain, but study of various examples shows that this was the case. Possibly an influx of New England craftsmen was the answer.

The classifying details of the Philadelphia school are the blunt-arrow design of the legs, the bold ball-turning of the stretchers, and the straightness of the front of the seat (*Illustration 85*). The leg usually starts with a ball- or knob-foot. Where stretchers and leg meet, there is a straight, round element while the rest of the leg is shaped slightly like a vase. In short the leg is without taper and of no noticeable variation in diameter. The stretchers have a boldly shaped ball or bulbousness in the centre, sometimes flanked by ring-turnings. The seat has a straight front, and the saddle shaping is pronounced and deeply concave. Sometimes so much so that over half the thickness of the seat has been cut away and the pommel in the centre of the front rises abruptly but with a pleasing curve. Also, in chairs from this area where the upper rail of the back terminates with knuckle-carved ends, these are usually deeply carved and well executed. To effect this, extra blocks were sometimes glued on the underside of the ends of the rail to provide the thickness needed for depth of carving. In the earlier low-back types the cresting of the centre of the back was accomplished with an upward curve, and the ends flared outward but were not knuckle-carved. In the treatment of the spindles, tapering is sometimes found, but usually not the bulbous enlargements used by New England chair-makers (*Drawing 27*).

With New England Windsors of all localities, taper and vase-shaping in leg-turnings is a common characteristic. In Connecticut and Rhode Island types it is bolder and more pronounced, and the diameter of the legs is greater, than in the types made in other parts of the area (*Illustration 88*). The leg typical of Connecticut starts at the foot with a plain turning and gradually tapers in reverse until well above the

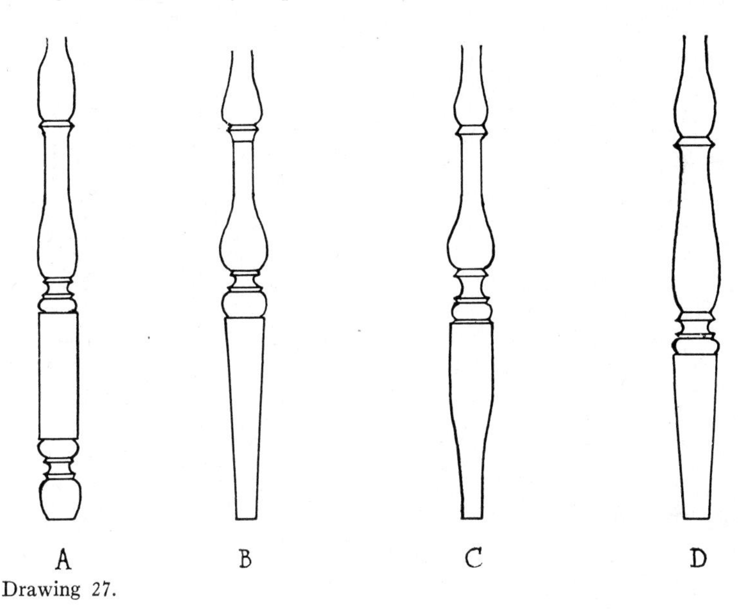

Drawing 27.

TYPICAL WINDSOR CHAIR LEGS

A, Philadelphia; B, general New England; C, Rhode Island; D, Connecticut.

level of the stretchers, where the straightness is broken by ring-turnings. Above this, vase-shaping carries out the finish to the point where the leg is inserted in the seat.

With the Rhode Island chair, the tapered foot is refined by a slight concave curve upward to the stretcher level. It is this fine distinction in the turning of the leg plus a deeper turning of the vase-work above the stretcher which differentiates Connecticut and Rhode Island work; while hard to describe, it is readily noticed when once understood.

All New England chairs are much alike in turning of stretchers. The bulbousness at the centre is gradual and is flanked by one or two ring turnings which are less deeply cut than with Philadelphia chairs (*Illustration 89*). Also the depression of the saddle-shaping of the seat was less, and the

A B

Illustration 88.

CONNECTICUT AND RHODE ISLAND WINDSORS COMPARED

A, Connecticut chair; B, Rhode Island variety. Compare the feet and leg turnings. A is late 18th Century; B, early 19th.

pommel so slight as sometimes to be only rudimentary. The front was curved rather than straight with a bold upward slant from the underside of the seat. In outline, these seats were oval rather than sharply U-shaped (*Drawing 28*). The treatment of the spindles also differs. Some fine examples

Illustration 89. *(Dr. George P. Coopernail)*

THREE NEW ENGLAND WINDSORS

They are all of the later 18th Century and are not of Connecticut or Rhode Island types.

have a bulbousness about a third of the distance from the seat. Others vary to shallow ring-turnings. The turnings of the heavier exterior spindles designed to support either arms or a comb-shaped upper rail, are of the vase-form and usually definitely related to that used in the legs.

In the bow-back chairs of this area are to be found the finest New England work. The skill with which these hoops were bent and the well-sprung curve that resulted gives them a quality that collectors have long appreciated. This is apparent both in the one-piece bow-back and in the hoop-back side-chairs.

The leg- and stretcher-turnings of the chairs produced in the New England back-country follow in detail those made in the larger towns but are less pronounced, and the saddle-seat is flatter. Such chairs were obviously made by men of lesser craftsmanship. In fact, while the turned parts and the U-shaped backpiece through which the spindles passed were made by journeymen, the rest of the chair and its assembling were often farm work. Chair parts were carried by general stores, and any man with mechanical skill could combine them with wood available on his farm and make his own Windsors. In spite of crude workmanship, grace and feeling for balance is apparent in proportion and line. Such a chair made in New Hampshire about 1800 has descended to me (*Illustration 90*). It is the sole survivor of a set of six and is here illustrated as typical of the work of a farmer who could turn his hand to chair-making if he wished.

In this chair, the legs, stretchers, and exterior spindles supporting the arms are of ash. The U-back is of quarter-sawed oak, the seat is whitewood, and the spindles and hoop are straight-grained white oak. Unfortunately this hoop was split at two points where spindles were inserted many years ago and was repaired by wrapping the breaks with pieces of leather. A good example of home workmanship even to the practical repair of the hoop.

These details of design and construction which indicate the

locality of production apply only to chairs made in the early and middle styles. Such individuality is not found with the rod-back and bamboo-turned types; so, unless there be other earmarks, locality of origin with these later styles is not readily told.

Some of the Windsors of this period were made in larger

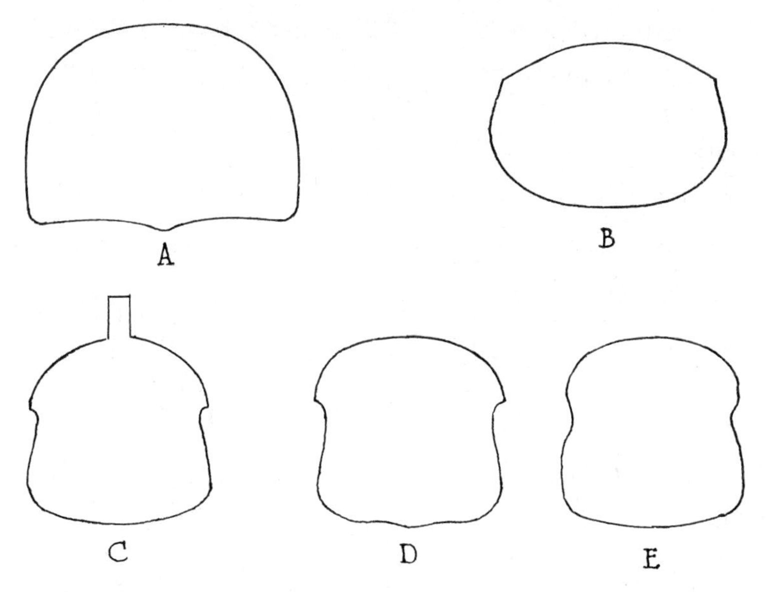

Drawing 28.

OUTLINE OF WINDSOR SEATS

A, Philadelphia; B, New England; C, brace back with tail piece; D, early hoop back; E, late side chair.

shops in such seaport towns as Salem and, like other furniture, shipped far and wide. Many of them went to the towns and plantations of the South. Occasionally a New England journeyman made a similar trip and established himself in a southern city, where he continued to make the types of chairs current in the northern town where his trade was learned. But these migrating workmen were relatively few, and most of the Windsors found below the Potomac may safely be considered as northern-made.

Illustration 90. *(Author's collection)*

A FARM–MADE WINDSOR

The turned parts were purchased, but the rest fashioned at home. Made at Ware, New Hampshire, between 1800 and 1815.

Windsors, like other much-used pieces of furniture, were sometimes made over to suit the fancy of a particular owner. One of the most common alterations was the addition of rockers.

About 1770 Benjamin Franklin, an ingenious printer and practical inventor as well as a man of real scientific attainments, devised the rocking-chair. He does not tell of this in his *Autobiography* as he does of his invention of the Franklin stove, but contemporary records are specific enough to credit Poor Richard with the idea.

The rocking-chair rapidly became an American favorite, and all sorts of chairs were modernized by shortening the legs and attaching the curved runners. Windsors lent themselves readily to such modification (*Illustration 91*). As a result many old chairs are found today either with rockers still attached or with legs about twelve inches long. Windsor chair seats were originally sixteen to eighteen inches from the ground, and little can be done about it. If the chair is otherwise good, leave the rockers, or replace them if missing. Attempts to splice the shortened legs are not successful. The slant of the legs makes it almost impossible to piece them so that they will be strong enough for use, which is the primary purpose of any chair, antique or otherwise.

In judging a writing Windsor, notice whether the tablet was part of the original or a later addition. Some Windsor armchairs were later converted to writing purposes by attaching a tablet. Study of the arm and its supports will tell the story. If original, there will be a logical relationship of the parts and their position. If the broad arm is a later addition, the way it is attached and its under-bracing will differ enough from the rest of the chair to indicate such work. This cannot be classed as faking but rather as honest modification done many years ago and in itself an interesting example of the practice of the day. Of course an original writing Windsor is more valuable than a converted one, but one of the most interesting chairs historically in America is a Windsor

Illustration 91. (*Metropolitan Museum of Art*)

EARLY 19TH CENTURY WINDSOR ROCKER

Here the back splats are fewer and arrow-shaped. The comb is heavy and without ears.

armchair to which a tablet was later added. This is the Thomas Jefferson chair mentioned earlier (*Illustration 84*). With no wish to detract from the importance of the piece but rather to get the facts, I studied this unique chair. Here was an opportunity to observe what was done in the Windsor period. My conclusions are that the tablet was attached at a later date and the work done, under Jefferson's directions, by a handy-man rather than the skilled craftsman who made the chair. Also the revolving base on which the seat rests appears to be later work. The outline of back and arm indicates a Windsor of about 1750, while the lower part seems to date twenty years later. Probably these changes were made in accordance with Jefferson's own ideas. Like Franklin, he was an originator of things mechanical as well as political. Not only is the chair unique for its historical associations, but the indications that it was reconstructed during the years of its use show that change and improvement were not confined to the machine age.

The injuries which Windsors have suffered from use and abuse are many and varied. There are splits or breaks of the hoop in bow-back types. A chair that has been knocked over will sometimes develop a break of the hoop at one of the points where a spindle end is inserted. Such breaks are also frequent in chairs left out-of-doors in rainy weather or stored in a damp place. Breaks may also occur in the U-arm immediately back of the end, at about the point of the first interior spindle. A split seat may result from excessive dampness. All such damages can be repaired by a skillful workman. Replacing missing spindles, stretchers, and legs comes in this category as well. It is an open question just how much repair work is justified. Repairing ordinary wear and tear is one thing; but when it reaches the point where it is original framework plus replacements of all or most of the ornamental features the border line has been crossed, and from a collector's point of view the result is a reconstructed Windsor of little value.

With fan- and comb-back chairs the volute scroll of the ears is a very important point, and one should be sure they are original. Sometimes such ears have been broken off. Sometimes combs originally plain are glorified by new carving to increase value. Neither replacement or added carving is desirable, and both should be avoided.

The Windsor idea as a plan of furniture design was too practical to be limited to arm and side chairs. Its adaptation to miniature chairs for little people was a logical development.

Among the children's chairs in the Windsor manner are to be found nearly all of the larger models. They were made with both long and short legs. With the Windsor highchairs a flat foot-rest was attached to the front legs, and a perfect example should have this feature unaltered. Among children's low-Windsors examples in practically all styles are extant and are often of the finest workmanship. They bear witness that children in the stern "seen but not heard" age were neither neglected nor forgotten by their elders. Producing adult things in miniature to please them was an established practice then as now. Moreover, the care with which these small pieces were made is in distinct contrast to the rather shoddy manufacturing methods apparent today with some of the furniture for children. In the Windsor highchair we find one very practical detail. The long legs are always given such an angle or rake that when occupied by a squirming two-year-old there was little possibility of the chair upsetting. In the low-chairs all details were executed with the same care as in full-size chairs. Considering the inherent sturdiness of this chair design, making them in miniature to receive the rough use children are prone to give their possessions was proper and fitting. It is surprising that more examples have not survived.

In enlarging the Windsor chair to a bench for two or more, the makers did not vary the design. The only change was lengthening the seat and adding more legs to hold the added

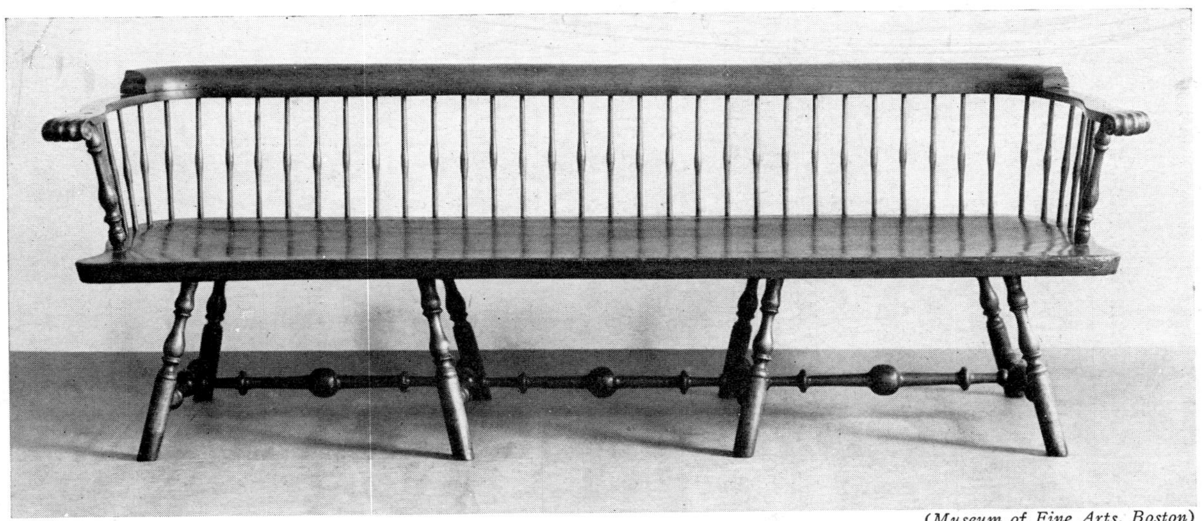

(Museum of Fine Arts, Boston)

Illustration 92.

A PHILADELPHIA WINDSOR BENCH

It is unusual in that it is made principally of curly maple. The stretcher turnings are typical of Pennsylvania work. *Ca.* 1760–1780.

weight of several occupants. Starting with the Philadelphia design of the earliest period and continuing down to the decadent, the settle was made in all of the accepted Windsor styles. (*Illustration 92.*)

They varied in size from love-seats for two to settees six feet long. Six and eight legs were usual, but some examples may be found with only four; others have as many as ten. In the abstract it would not seem that a graceful piece would result from adapting the Windsor chair to settee proportions. Actually most settees are pieces of definite appeal as to line and proportion. In fact the meeting-room bench with all its plainness and lack of ornamental detail has more merit than its companion in decadence, the fire-house single chair. There is a simple dignity and honesty of structure about it which in the single chair is mere clumsiness.

Another variation of the Windsor idea was the footstool. It was usually a simple affair with three or four plainly turned legs and a very simple flat top. The old hand-wrought milking stool also is a crude example of Windsor construction.

From the footstool to the making of that rare piece, a Windsor table, was but a step. Here three or four legs with a single or double tier of stretchers provided the underbody. (*Illustration 93.*) The top was either square or round. The height of such pieces indicates a use akin to the present-day coffee table rather than a substitute for a table of more orthodox design. They were largely made for taverns and public houses, and only a very few examples have survived. I have studied many advertisements of old Windsor chair-makers but I have never found one which mentions such tables. Obviously their making was occasional and only to meet special demand.

From all of the Windsor forms that developed, the versatility and skill of the men who followed this branch of cabinet-making is clearly shown. As a piece of furniture the Windsor, whether it was a chair, stool, or settee, had three distinct attributes—comfort, good looks, and sturdiness—which commended it to popular esteem. As a result the Windsor persisted beyond any other type. Even today Windsors are made not

Illustration 93. *(Pennsylvania Museum, Philadelphia)*

A RARE WINDSOR TABLE

The raised edge of the top is a feature taken over from the dish-top candle stand. *Ca.* 1800–1810.

half so much as reproductions as because they are comfortable, will give good service and stand hard wear.

During the Windsor century, the makers were constantly

modifying details of construction and adapting the idea to new uses. These variations speak loudly of the popularity of Windsor chairs in America. The immigrant was absorbed with surprising speed, naturalized, and became an important and representative citizen.

CHAPTER SEVEN

SOFAS AND SETTLES

SOFAS and settles are simply chair forms grown larger. From the simple bench of the 17th Century grew the settle, and from the upholstered armchair of our Chippendale, Hepplewhite, Sheraton, and Empire years, the sofa with earmarks of these succeeding styles. In fact, one can properly think of settles and sofas as Cinderella relations. Both were furniture forms brought to this country from England and points east. The former and elder was a plain workaday piece designed for location beside the large fireplace which was both cookstove and heating plant for the primitive Puritan century house (*Illustration 94*). The high back of the settle and enclosing sides which usually extended to the floor and replaced feet, served not only to lean against but to deflect chilly drafts. Seated in it, either at the side or directly in front of a fireplace, the 17th Century American could roast himself to a turn while the far corners of the room remained freezing-cold. Again we see the practicality of the furniture made during the first hundred years that white men occupied the former hunting and fishing preserves of the American Indians.

In fact, as far as the settle was concerned, the Anglo-Saxon developers of the United-States-to-be continued to make it all through the early 18th Century as they pioneered farther inland. From the first to last these pieces differed little in line or design. They were simply expedient carry-overs, and it is next to impossible to state of a particular settle whether it was made during the Sixteen Hundreds or in a remote new settlement during the next hundred years. But as it moved out of the more effete older towns to those where neighbors a mile or even five miles away were downright close, its place was taken by the sofa, in which upholstery for seat, back, and generally arms was more to the fancy of the less hardy who preferred to remain among the comforts and refinements of life.

In structure, the settle was the bench made of boards with

Illustration 94. *(Gallery of Fine Arts, Yale Univ.)*

A PRIMITIVE PINE SETTLE

It is of late 17th or early 18th Century origin.

sides and back added. In general the only effort at ornamentation was cutting the upper parts of the sides in a simple curve. The seat was not deep, nor was the back often given a backward cant to make it more comfortable. Straight and boxlike was the accepted pattern, and plain pine boards were the material. In a few instances the back was given an architectural treatment by replacing the vertical boards, tongued and grooved together to make them breeze-proof, with simple wainscot paneling that probably matched the room in which the piece stood. This and a central bracket built up from the seat as a stand on which to place a candle or rush-wicked lamp for evening reading were all the refinements applied. A plain piece built from memory of kindred ones in English farm cottages, it began and ended. The Carolean and suc-

Illustration 95. (*Metropolitan Museum of Art*)

A QUEEN ANNE SOFA

This piece was made in Philadelphia between 1730 and 1745.

ceeding styles affected it not at all. An Elizabethan yeoman it remained to the very end. By the middle of the 18th Century, when people demanded something more elaborate, our cabinetmakers were ready to produce for them its more aristocratic younger brother, the sofa. This they did all up and down the coastal towns and farming areas with skill and an eye appreciative of both curves and straight lines.

The earliest sofas apparently were made in Philadelphia, which during the fifty years before the Declaration of Independence, was a curious combination of the simplicity that ruled the lives of members of the Society of Friends and a luxurious and pompous scale of living that mirrored London. It was the colonial capital of wealth and fashion. Southern planters came there for the season, and all in all, despite the Quaker predominance, it was as gay and festive a place as could be found along the Atlantic seaboard. Knowing that the sofa was an accepted piece of drawing-room furniture in England and had been since the Restoration, by the closing years of the Queen Anne style cabinetmakers and upholsterers conspired to meet this customer demand. (*Illustration 95.*)

So they made sofas with walnut feet and legs, cabriole with Dutch feet for the two front ones and two or three plain backward-flaring ones for the rear. All the rest was upholstered. The back was formed with arching curves at the top and earlike volutes at the upper corners not so different from the wing chairs then being made. The arms, too, followed this pattern save that they were generally given an outward roll to balance the ears of the back. Still the back was of chair height, making it easy to see that these first examples were sprung directly from the upholstered easy-chair just as were the love-seats from the armchairs with more of the wooden framework visible.

With this introduction into polite society the sofa spread up and down the country. During the Chippendale years it was as a rule made with plain square legs and stretchers of mahogany and the upper part all textile-covered (*Illustration 96*). The back was a cyma curve higher at the centre than at the ends—camel's hump, some call it—and the arms flared outward like those of a wing chair. Chippendale sofas, unlike those of the Queen Anne style, were generally a third or quarter lower than the upholstered chairs of the period. During the twenty years of Hepplewhite little change was

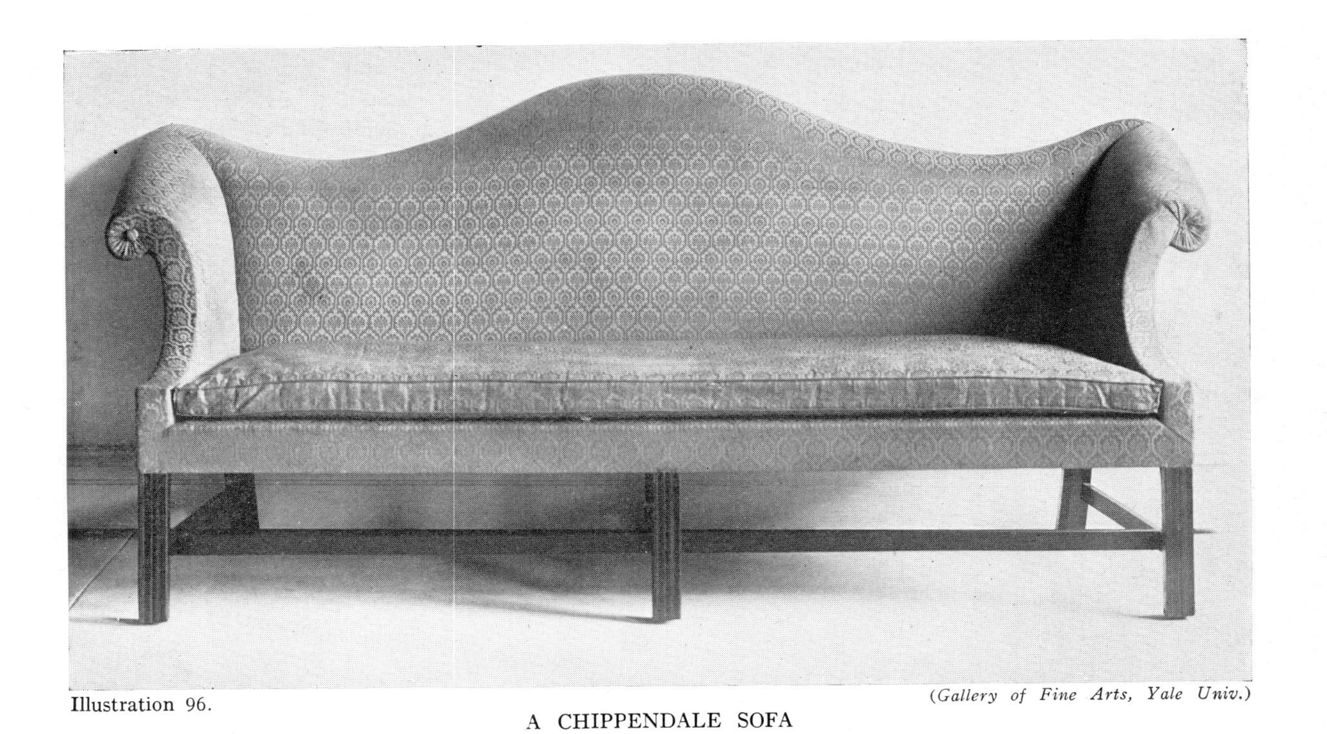

Illustration 96. *(Gallery of Fine Arts, Yale Univ.)*

A CHIPPENDALE SOFA

It is either of Newburyport, Massachusetts; or Portsmouth, New Hampshire, origin. Made *ca.* 1800–1810.

Illustration 97. *(Ginsburg & Levy, Inc.)*

A NEW ENGLAND HEPPLEWHITE SOFA

The back is much lower than the Queen Anne and Chippendale types. *Ca.* 1785–1795.

made in construction and lines. (*Illustration 97.*) Six tapered legs without stretchers replaced the square ones of Chippendale, but the shaping and outline of the upper body remained practically unchanged.

By 1800, the plan of sofa design came under the Sheraton influence which, as it developed during the next quarter-century, produced the finest and most artistic of these pieces made in America. It was a gradual progress, however, to the fine examples of McIntire and Phyfe. The 1800 to 1810 type was characterized by eight mahogany legs, the front four reeded and turned as were those of other pieces of this period, and the back four square and canted away as with all of the chairs from the Queen Anne through the Empire. At the front corners, the reeded legs often continued upward to short wooden arms that soon disappeared beneath the upholstery fabric (*Illustration 98*).

There were two types of design for seat, back, and covered arms. One had a slightly arching back, that is, a single curving sweep extending from one front leg to the other which gave the back edge of the seat an arclike curve that balanced the slight swell of the front frame. The entire upper body was covered with a textile fabric, and the only ornamental woodwork visible was in the legs, the extensions at the front corners and the short length of arm. In this design, we see the French influence of the Louis Seize period, but with curves much simplified. In the other design, curves, except for downward ones of the arms which are gradual and shallow, are eliminated. The top line of the back is almost straight, and those of the seat completely so. The front legs are extended upward to meet the arms, and these have an upper edge of mahogany extending to the back, which is reeded to match the reeding of the four front legs. At the seat level the corner legs are square, and the front surface decorated with an oblong inlay of light-colored wood. Other than this the upper body was upholstered similar to the other style.

From these two sprang the better known sofas of the

Illustration 98. *(Gallery of Fine Arts, Yale Univ.)*

AN EARLY SHERATON SOFA

It is either of Newburyport, Massachusetts; or Portsmouth, New Hampshire, origin. Made *ca.* 1800–1810.

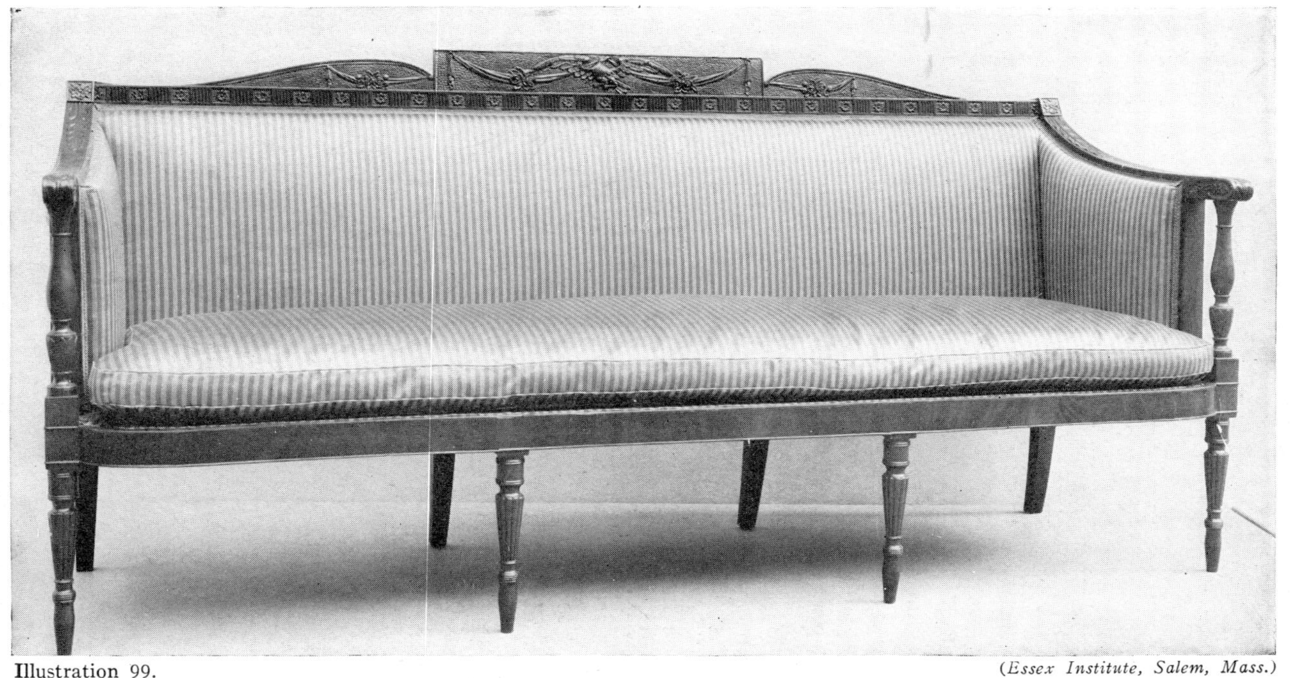

Illustration 99. *(Essex Institute, Salem, Mass.)*

A SHERATON SOFA MADE BY MCINTYRE

Formerly all fine work of Salem origin was automatically ascribed to him. Now we know there were other craftsmen of ability working there at the same time. *Ca.* 1810.

1810–1825 period. Here the rectilinear plane was followed. The top of the back was no longer arched but a straight line, and on it was placed a cross-member of carved mahogany connected to the upper edges of the ends, which were reeded cyma curves extending from the back to where they joined the upper extensions of the corner front legs. Much fine carving ornamented the cross-member of the back. Phyfe kept this piece rectangular in outline and divided it into panels. His usual practice was to decorate the centre one with a draped festoon, and the outer ones with sheaves of arrows bound at the centre with an encircling ribbon whose bows and ends stood out boldly as part of the design.

In the McIntire type—he seems also to have made earlier sofas of Hepplewhite lines, which Phyfe did not—the wooden cross-member of the back was more elaborate in outline (*Illustration 99*). Its bottom edge was straight, while the upper one had a central section that was also straight and somewhat higher than the rest. This was flanked on either side by swelling arched members which at their widest are not equal to the panel. The decoration for them is a drapery festoon while that of the central panel has two festoons that hang pendent on either side of an eagle with outspread wings. The background was finished in a pebble effect, for which this Salem artist seemed to have a great fondness. Beneath the cresting, the straight line of the back was ornamented by a dado in which incised, carved rosettes alternated with blocks of reeding. The upper surface of the arms generally had an acanthus-leaf carving in place of the reeding, and the front legs, though sometimes turned, are reeded. McIntire died in 1811, and his son, who continued the business, in 1819. Therefore, unlike Phyfe, they were not part of the gradual shift from this graceful Sheraton to the French Directoire and thence to American Empire.

As for the New York master, a detailed account of the various designs which he employed in making sofas would make a small book in itself. So we can only touch the high spots. (*Illustration 100.*) Some of his pieces instead of being upholstered were finished with cane for back, seats, and arms.

A

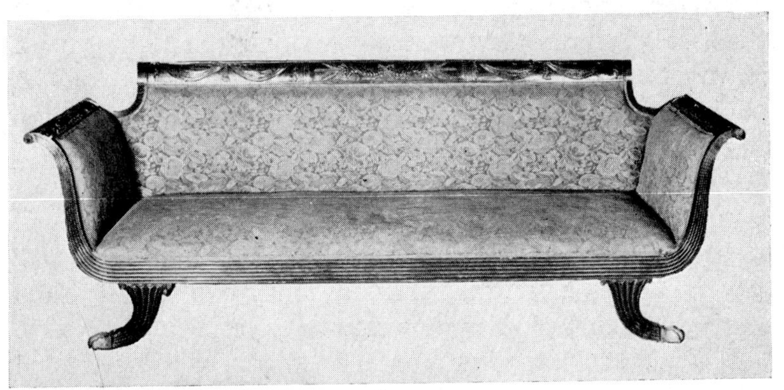

Illustration 100. B

TWO PHYFE SOFAS

A, Sheraton style with cane back, arms, and seat. B, Directoire style with reeded front and brass claw-feet. Both antedate 1825.

When this was done, the entire framework was mahogany, and the outlines and ornamentation practically as described. In another style, for the eight short legs he substituted a trestlework of curving arcs which gives the piece the look of an old-fashioned wooden bridge supported by timber arches. We do not feel that this was one of his happiest furniture thoughts. On the other hand, he made another sofa in this Directoire mode quite as graceful as the Sheraton. This had a low arched back, enclosed out-scrolled arms with the face of both arms and seat of fluted mahogany forming a much widened U. The whole was supported by four concave legs of hornlike curve terminating in brass claw-feet. In such a piece he showed his mastery of curved lines that complemented instead of contradicting each other.

Because Phyfe, by the superiority of his work and the volume production of his shops with their hundred or more workmen, was the leading craftsman, other men working in the same city and probably in the same manner have been lost in the shuffle. Possibly some of the sofas we now attribute to Phyfe never saw his shop. For example, in the *New York Evening Post* for 1817, the advertisement of Davis and Wheatley appeared about thrice a week for most of that year. It was illustrated with a copper-plate engraving of a sofa that in line and detail is what we now concede to be Phyfe. Is it not probable that this firm, whose shop on Broadway opposite St. Paul's Chapel was less than a block and a half away from that of the renowned cabinetmaker, may have made a good percentage of the Sheraton sofas credited to Phyfe? Since seeing this newspaper bid for patronage I have made a number of inquiries in likely quarters for sofas bearing the label of this partnership. As yet none have come to light. Although the firm was sufficiently advertising-minded to make consistent use of daily newspaper space, either it did not complete it by labeling its wares, or in the less enlightened years repair men may have scraped its labels away as dirty stickers of no importance.

As our Empire style gained the ascendency, Phyfe changed his style of sofa, and not for the better. The reeded legs and the concave ones both gave way for carved claw-feet with

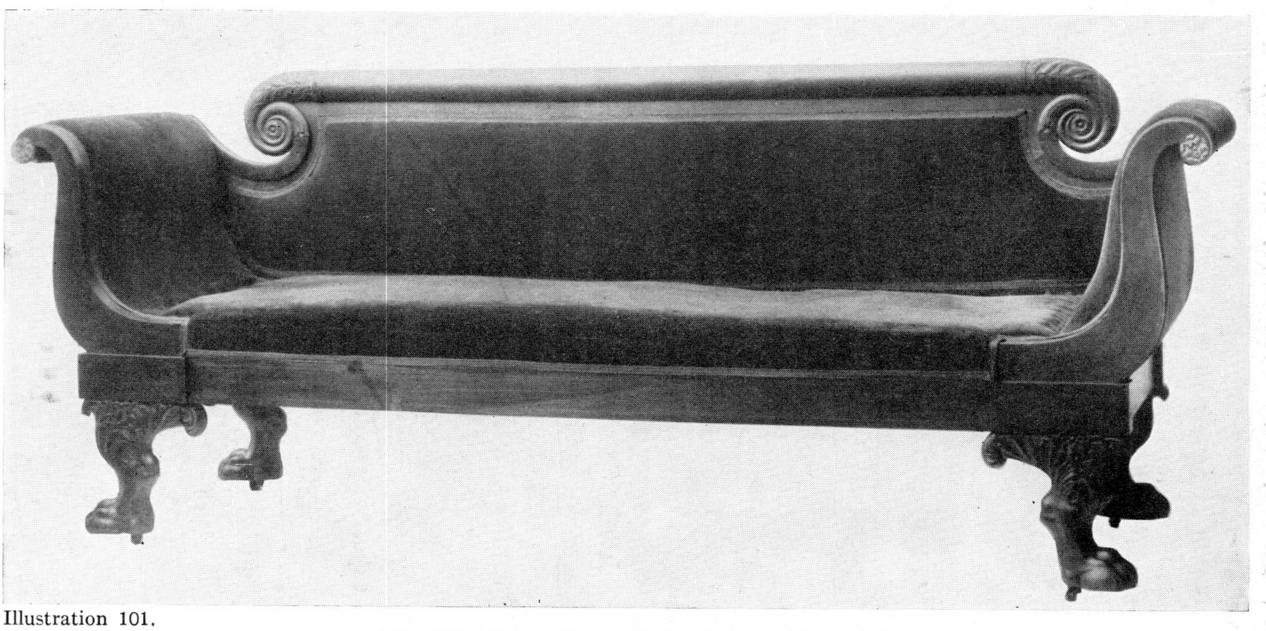

Illustration 101.

AN EMPIRE SOFA DONE WITH RESTRAINT

It is in the 1825–1835 mode.

an element of carving to simulate hair above, and cornucopia-curved ends replaced the simpler and more graceful earlier details (*Illustration 101*). The back became heavier. In short, it was his attempt to give the public what it wanted. Such sofas at their best—with their wealth of carved ornamentation and brass mounts, horn-curved arms, and backs ending in downward volutes—are, considering the heaviness characteristic of the period, pieces with merit. While not of the quality of preceding eras, they are worth acquiring at a reasonable price.

Some people seem to be firm in the conviction that, because American Sheraton sofas of the Phyfe-McIntire designs bring several hundred dollars each, a similar price is proper for an American Empire made by some one of the ten thousand cabinetmakers then working. Of course this is an unwarranted appraisal. Even an Empire sofa bearing all the earmarks of Phyfe production is worth but a fraction of one that is Sheraton in line and detail. So the wise collector will be chary of buying the former at too high a price.

As the years went on, sofas, in common with other pieces, were made with diminishing art and increasing bulk. Those with back in three panels and the front a wriggling serpentine track, are Empire crossed with Victorian, and, although I have one acquired by inheritance and kept for sentiment's sake, I should not expect any collector in his right senses to buy it.

CHAPTER EIGHT

CUPBOARDS, DRESSERS, AND SIDEBOARDS

SEVENTEENTH CENTURY Americans were trenchermen in the real sense of the word. Their homes, save in rare instances, were bare of silver, glass, or ceramics. Except for a little pewter, their table appointments were wooden trenchers and bowls and leathern mugs for the small beer, cider, or stronger drink. Not until the 18th Century was there any need for cupboards to hold Lowestoft and Stiegel glass, or sideboards for plate. During the first century in this country, however, there were opulent families who had a piece of furniture every bit as imposing as the most elaborate sideboard. This was the press cupboard. It was placed in the room where meals were served just as was the sideboard a century later.

In England, from the time of Elizabeth until the Tudor tradition in furniture design had been completely supplanted, there were two types of ornamental cupboards: the court and the press. The former does not designate an unusually fine piece fit for a monarch but is simply the French word for "short." In fact, a cupboard without base intended to be placed on a trestle or other supporting piece of furniture. In the latter years of their production these short cupboards were sometimes made with supporting legs of their own, but this space was not enclosed. If any were made in America or brought here by the early colonists, they have long since disappeared, for not one has been unearthed during the past quarter-century although collectors and dealers have combed the country time and again.

The same group of craftsmen who produced the Connecticut chests also made a few press cupboards (*Illustration 102*).

Competent specialists in American furniture of the 17th Century now hold that not over seventy-five examples of

Illustration 102. *(Gallery of Fine Arts, Yale Univ.)*

A 17TH CENTURY PRESS CUPBOARD

Pieces of this sort, while fundamentally Elizabethan in manner, were made in New England *ca.* 1650–1680.

native-made press cupboards are extant, and probably fewer. As to rarity, they are about in the class with Gutenberg Bibles. Made of oak, with other native woods used for the out-of-sight parts, they were ornamented about as were the elaborate chests of the same period. Some were decorated with carved panels in the sunflower and tulip motifs. Others had drawer and door fronts embellished with molding in geometric patterns. All had split baluster and egg-shaped bosses. The upper third was a cupboard with central door and diagonal sides placed beneath an overhanging cornice supported at the corners by baluster-turned columns that rested on the top of the carcass proper. The latter either was developed as a single closet with a paneled door or was fitted with drawers, usually three of uniform size. Some of these pieces were provided with turnip feet; in others the stiles at the corners projected downward to provide the necessary support to raise the piece six or eight inches from the floor. In either type the construction is that of the Connecticut chest—panels, stiles, rails, with red, black, and other paint colors used for finish.

Just as a chest of this type occasionally turns up unrecognized, in some out-of-the-way location, possibly a press cupboard may be encountered under like circumstances. Therefore, although the average collector may not expect ever to see such a piece outside of the imprisoning walls of some museum, it *might* be worth his while to know what it is, and what it looks like. The years of the American press cupboard were from 1660 to 1680, and its habitat was where the handsome chests of these years were made, the Connecticut Valley from Hadley south, and possibly more easterly parts of Massachusetts. As its name implies, it was probably used for storage of linen.

By approximately 1675 more pewter plates and basins, ewers, and tankards and other pieces began to be made in the colonies or brought from the old country. Also there was a rudimentary production of slip-ware bowls, large plates, pottery jugs and jars. By 1635, Richard Graves, a turbulent fellow always at odds with authority, was following the pewterer's trade in Salem. Six years later that same town boasted a potter in the person of William Vincent or Vinson, who was a

Illustration 103.

AN EARLY 18TH CENTURY DRESSER

This shows how many pieces look when first found and before repairs have been made.

householder, quite properly, in potter's field. With metallic and ceramic table furnishings of native make available in other settlements up and down the Atlantic coast, it was logical for housewives to demand some place to store prized things of this sort where they would show. The earliest arrangements were plain shelves placed one above another.

From this primitive beginning sprang the dressers, cupboards, and corner cupboards that soon were being made with distinct, if restrained, ornamental detail. Many of them were just rectangular boxlike affairs with an upper and a lower door concealing tiers of plain shelves within. Made of pine, they were footless and devoid of decorative elements. Later the doors were given panel treatment, and sometimes a cornice molding was added to give the top finish and bulb-feet raised the piece a little from the floor. Even later the upper doors were dispensed with, the opening given scallops, and the revealed shelves improved similarly. At best, such a piece was neither as capacious nor as noticeable as the much more popular dresser.

The latter came from the west of England, where Owen Glendower once disputed the independence of Wales to the distinct discomfort of Britain's Henry IV. The Welsh had a name for this piece, *cwpwedd tridarn.* But "dresser," it was always called by the less agile-tongued Anglo-Saxons who adopted it in Tudor times and in both the Old and the New World continued to make and use it until the close of the 18th Century (*Illustration 103*).

In line and structure it was a wide, shallow piece of furniture approximating room height. The bottom half, somewhat deeper than the rest, was like the press cupboard inclosed. Here an element of drawers was located at the top, and beneath that closet space made accessible by doors. The top of this carcass might be used as a serving table, and above it rose a series of open shelves for storage and display of sundry pewter, earthenware dishes, and the like.

In America this dresser was nearly always a pine piece and

somewhat architectural in its dimensions and ornamentation. The drawer-fronts were universally plain, and some dressers even lacked drawers entirely; the doors were simple paneled ones held in place by iron H-hinges. Often there were no feet for a bottom finish. But above it was different. The dish

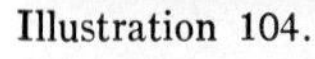

Illustration 104. *(Gallery of Fine Arts, Yale Univ.)*

A B

TWO 18TH CENTURY CORNER CUPBOARDS

A, Removable. B, Built-in.

shelves and the sides supporting them were given scallop-cutting in simple balancing curves. This with the well-executed but not too heavy cornice made the dresser a piece of furniture that had to be noticed when present. There was good showmanship in making this display piece decorative. Department store executives now recognize that the most attractive merchandise shown in unattractive cases is unnoticed by the passing throng, while distinctly mediocre things shown in cases with a nicety of line and decoration attract attention far out of proportion to their merit. So with these dressers. Whether the old craftsmen realized that the decorative treatment which they gave their otherwise plain board construction would enhance the beauty of the housewives' pewter and dishes, matters not. The result was the same. Certainly colonial women appreciated the dresser for both use and display so thoroughly that it was made in all localities by both cabinetmakers and carpenters, who fashioned them in keeping with the paneling and trim of the rooms in which they were to stand.

From the dresser which stood flat against a side or end wall it was but a step to the corner closet (*Illustration 104*). This, as its name connotes, was a piece occupying a right-angle meeting of walls. Its front was set on the diagonal, and its shelves were triangular. As a furniture form it came into general use in America with the Georgian years and continued through the Sheraton, a few being made in our Empire style. Structurally it was in two parts like the dresser. The lower contained a closet with a solid paneled door, while the upper might be with or without doors.

In earlier forms the doors were wooden with panels nicely formed, and in later styles glass, cut in diamond or other shapes and held in place by bar moldings of wood, was often employed. The opening itself was frequently arched and flanked on either side by moldings or pilasters that extended down to the base. Many of these cupboards were built-in and formed an integral part of the wall treatment, whether paneled or plastered. Others were made movable. Frequently the back wall was shaped in a curve or had its right-angled sharpness replaced by a diagonal board parallel to the front. Either treatment was intended to make room for the corner post of the house frame, which projected four to eight inches into the room. Another refinement fairly prevalent was to give

Illustration 105. *(William Stuart Walcott, Jr., Esq.)*

A HEPPLEWHITE SIDEBOARD

Made 1790 by Mills & Deming of New York.

the cupboard at the top of the inside a hemispherical curve that combined well with the quarter-round sweep of the back. The front edges of the shelves frequently were cut in a receding curve, which sometimes had a central round projection as an ideal spot to place, for display but not safety, an especially fine bit of china or pewter.

The design of doors and surrounding framework consisted of architectural pilasters, arches with keystones, and moldings of the period. Both soft and hard woods were considered proper material for these pieces. The built-in types were always of pine, while the movable ones might be of this soft wood, native hard wood, or mahogany. Very few corner cupboards that could be taken along when a family changed homes without tearing out a corner of the room were made before the Sheraton and Empire years, and of course each individual cupboard is dated by the architectural style of its design. To judge by the number still in existence, they were very popular and were made by cabinetmakers and carpenters alike from Maine to Georgia and as far inland as there were towns in which the niceties of living were appreciated.

American sideboards were first made in the Hepplewhite manner and characterized by slender legs like those of the tables (*Illustration 105*). Generally there were six, the front being equipped with two extra which served as accents to divide the central section from those that flanked it at either end. The wood was mahogany with door and drawer fronts finished in fine crotch-grained veneer. Likewise, lines of inlay and ornamental medallions, festoons, and pendent husks of marquetry were used for ornamentation. These sideboards might be square of front, serpentine, or have a sweeping curve. A typical arrangement was three drawers immediately beneath the top, the largest in the centre and smaller ones at each side. Beneath, there might be closets in either end section and two more drawers, one under the other, in the centre portion; or this space could be given over to a closet provided with double doors. In those with the serpentine front the common practice was to set the additional legs on the diagonal which served to accentuate the angles of the serpentine. Some with straight fronts had a level of drawers, and beneath this a large closet with tambour doors.

Such sideboards were made from about 1790 to 1800 and

Illustration 106. (*Ginsburg & Levy, Inc.*)

A SHERATON SIDEBOARD

Although it is unlabeled, details of workmanship indicate that it was made by John Seymour & Son of Boston about 1790.

were, in my opinion, the finest pieces produced by our craftsmen working in the Hepplewhite style. Two outstanding sideboard makers whose labeled pieces have been found within the past few years, were Benjamin Frothingham of Charlestown, Massachusetts, who won both a major's commission and Washington's friendship during the Revolution, and a New York partnership, Mills and Deming. The latter made a number of very fine sideboards that have been recently located in

Connecticut. The one they made for Governor Oliver Wolcott distinctly deserves to be considered as the high point in American workmanship for this piece and period.

When the Sheraton style displaced that of George Hepplewhite and his wife Dame Alice, sideboard making was not

Illustration 107.

A SOUTHERN HUNTING BOARD

The wood is walnut. It was made either in Georgia or in South Carolina after 1820. As the returned hunters stood around the board to eat, such pieces were always taller than the conventional sideboard. This one is forty-nine inches high.

fundamentally altered as far as American craftsmen were concerned (*Illustration 106*). The main outlines remained much the same, as with the chests of drawers; but the tapered leg was replaced by the turned and reeded one, which might be all but disengaged from the body. Inlay was replaced in some by a little carving on the upper ends of the legs, and the whole piece was a few inches taller than the earlier ones. In two points innovations were made: A pair of deep but narrow drawers shaped to accommodate bottles of spirituous beverages were incorporated in the arrangement of drawers and

Illustration 108.

A SMALL NEW ENGLAND SIDEBOARD OF SHERATON LINES

The central cupboard was designed for storage of silver plate and the flanking deep drawers for bottles. Typical of the work done about 1810.

closets; and the central section was made shallower vertically than those at either end, and the space below was finished with an arclike curve.

So much for the urban-made sideboards of both periods. With those of rural make there were some slight differences.

In the southern states the Hepplewhite style was applied to a simple piece of rectilinear form known as a hunting board (*Illustration 107*). It might have a pair of drawers, but the rest was given over to closet space. Usually made in walnut

Illustration 109. (*Ginsburg & Levy, Inc.*)

AN AMERICAN EMPIRE SIDEBOARD

It is of New York make and probably from the Phyfe shops. When repaired, the tambour work was found to be backed with newspapers bearing the date 1816.

or other native woods, the whole effect was pure plantation in simplicity of outline and workmanship.

While the approximate length of elaborate sideboards of city make was six feet, those fabricated in New England villages were much like the chest of drawers in size, line, and design (*Illustration 108*). But bottle drawers and other features proclaimed that they were designed for dining rooms rather than bedrooms. They were made in mahogany and native hard woods. Some of the best combined mahogany with fancy maple, either curly or bird's-eye.

For all of these pieces, the hardware was like that of the chests of drawers then being made. Some very fine city examples had drawer-pulls of ivory instead of brass, but this was not a general practice. Because of their size, only people living in mansions had rooms large enough for the big sideboards of either style, and so these pieces were not made in such quantity as chests of drawers. Because of their sectional production, southern hunting boards are not overplentiful either. Similarly the reduced-size sideboards of rural New England, since they do not require large floor space, have a demand far exceeding the supply. Consequently the collector who would buy a sideboard of Hepplewhite or Sheraton design, city- or country-made, must prepare to pay the piper.

During the Empire years, the sideboard met about the same fate as the chest of drawers (*Illustration 109*). Clumsy columns and pilasters, carved claw-feet, too heavy lines and dimensions, generally resulted. Some few had dignity, balance, and restraint; but more often craftsmen in trying to meet the public demand overdid the design, and the results were florid and pompous to a hopeless degree. Anyone unfortunate enough to own such a piece is almost in the position of the soft-hearted Arab who invited his camel into his tent. In most cases it fairly fills the dining room and overpowers everything else there.

CHAPTER NINE

HIGHBOYS AND LOWBOYS

In the making of the twin pieces highboys and lowboys, American craftsmen left those of England far behind. This was undoubtedly due to the fact that the vogue for both in the old country lasted only from the Restoration years to the beginning of the Georgian period. In America, on the contrary, the days of their years were more than fourscore, and from their primitive beginning about 1690 they were in high favor throughout the colonies. Did Deacon So-and-So in Old Deerfield acquire a highboy, his neighbors were straightway treated to sour looks by their women-folk and pointed remarks about how bare the space between the two windows looked until they capitulated and ordered one of the coveted pieces.

Indeed, right up to the time of the Boston Tea Party, cabinetmakers all the way from Maine to the Chesapeake made these pieces in quantity, to judge from the many examples that have survived. Yet after this patriotic if lawless fancy-dress escapade, highboy and lowboy patterns seem to have been folded up and put away if not destroyed. Were they classed as a Tory style and therefore displeasing to a public that had "Taxation without representation is tyranny" for its theme song? or, in the general unrest of the time, were they considered simply too expensive? Whatever the cause of their fall from favor, it is an occurrence to be regretted. If Americans could adapt the lines and ornamentation of Chippendale as successfully as they did in the Van Pelt highboy referred to earlier (*Illustration 3*), what might they have achieved in the tradition of either Hepplewhite or Sheraton!

Were this a botanical treatise, *Family Arca, species Puer Altus* would be a proper heading, as a pine piece in the Bolles Collection at the Metropolitan Museum shows very clearly

Illustration 110. (*Metropolitan Museum of Art*)

SMALL PAINTED CHEST ON FRAME

This shows the 17th Century beginnings of highboy making in America.

the elementary highboy being evolved from the chest by the simple expedient of placing it on a framework base of the same lines as those used for the first desks and tavern tables (*Illustration 110*). In this particular piece, beneath the well

Illustration 111. A B *(Gallery of Fine Arts, Yale Univ.)*

WILLIAM AND MARY HIGHBOY AND LOWBOY

Both are of walnut with mounts of the period. The highboy has burl walnut veneer on drawer fronts and the front of the lower section. New England workmanship, 1700–1710. The lowboy is of New England origin, 1700–1720.

that is accessible by raising the lid, there is a single drawer. Likewise the apron of the base has one. The legs, feet, and the scalloped stretchers are distinctly of William and Mary design and indicate that the piece was made during the last twenty years of the 17th Century. Whether this actually is the first of its type made here is beside the point. It is the first American step in the design of a piece which was to be followed speedily by many refinements both of line and of construction.

Drawing 29.

The trumpet leg and bulbous foot of William and Mary highboy.

The first years of the next century saw this accomplished, and saw also the lowboy which was achieved by replacing the chest with a table top. These William and Mary pieces, whether high or low, had the trumpet leg and bulbous foot typical of the period (*Illustration* 111). The stretcher was always flat and usually shaped with cyma curves corresponding to those of the apron. With highboys, this was oblong in outline, while with lowboys, two diagonals forming a cross or X were usual. For the taller piece, six legs was the general practice. The lower ones as a rule were provided with only four (*Drawing* 29). The design of skirt and arrangement of drawers in it were always the same in either case. The front and sides of the skirt were always cut away in arching cyma curves, and the edge finished with a narrow cocklebead molding, which was likewise employed for finish on the fronts of the two deep drawers on the right and left as well as the shallower one located in the centre above the more pronounced arch of the skirt.

Lowboys were from twenty-eight to thirty-two inches high. Their tops always overhung the base about three inches, and the front and side edges were finished with rounding thumb molding. Two turned, pendent finials pointing downward were always placed at the base of the central arch of the apron at

Illustration 112. (*Israel Sack*)

A SINO–AMERICAN HIGHBOY

It was made in New England about 1720 and lacquered in China.

the points where in highboys occurred the additional legs.

In the William and Mary highboys as in all others, the upper section was two to four inches narrower than the lower, and this break was accomplished by the use of a double tier of molding which was the same in elements as that used for the cornice, which was always flat. Bonnet tops did not appear until the Queen Anne years, and their most elaborate development came during the Chippendale period. The usual arrangement of drawers in the William and Mary style was four tiers, increasing in depth as they descended. The general practice was to divide the uppermost section to accommodate two drawers of half the width of those below. Both highboys and lowboys during this period, which as far as they were concerned extended from 1700 to about 1720, were equipped with the characteristic tear-drop handles, and whether in New England or farther South, walnut was the wood principally used. Some of these pieces were made with very beautiful burl walnut veneer on the drawer faces and front skirt of the base while more of them were produced from straight-grained walnut. Others were made of pine and painted either in a single color or with a background and a floral design in several colors. Very rare is a William and Mary highboy or lowboy of maple, and rarer still is one done in Chinese lacquer (*Illustration 112*). Such a piece was made in the colonies and then shipped to the East to be ornamented by Celestial workmen. Probably several years were consumed in traveling to and from Canton, famous at home and abroad for the skill and quality of its craftsmen working in this medium. When it finally did come to rest it was undoubtedly in the home of a ship-owning family.

By 1720, the William and Mary style in the highboy and its companion piece of table height had spent itself, and American craftsmen forsook it for Queen Anne lines and details. Initially this shift was marked by the cabriole leg, pad-foot, and stretcherless form of this new style (*Illustration 113*). The taller pieces, of course, could no longer be built with six legs. Walnut continued to be the favored wood, and the drawer arrangement and scalloping of the skirt in an arclike curve was still adhered to; but the highboys were now a little taller. Six feet was the general height, with five drawers of increasing depth in the upper half. With some, the top-

Illustration 113. *(American Art Assn.–Anderson Galleries)*

AN EARLY QUEEN ANNE LOWBOY

The wood is walnut, and it was probably made in Pennsylvania, 1730–1750.

drawer space was modified to accommodate two or even three small narrow drawers. In the lower section the common practice was to place a single drawer nearly as wide as the piece at the top and a grouping of three others beneath it. Of these the central one was shallow but somewhat wider than the two

A B C

Illustration 114. (Gallery of Fine Arts, Yale Univ.)

TYPICAL QUEEN ANNE HIGHBOYS

A, New England curly maple, 1730–1750. B, Connecticut, 1730–1745, with flat top and full sunburst carved ornament in skirt. C, Maple with bonnet top and half sunburst carving on both top and bottom, 1740–1760.

that flanked it, which were approximately twice its depth. This plan allowed for the arching curve of the skirt and utilized the space of its front surface admirably. Pendent finials, as in the William and Mary lowboys, were generally placed at the low points of the arches of the apron. Some of these pieces were made with drawer fronts and skirt finished in crotch or burl veneer and the drawer openings outlined with a cocklebead or other molding. The cornice was made of molding members somewhat more elaborate than in the

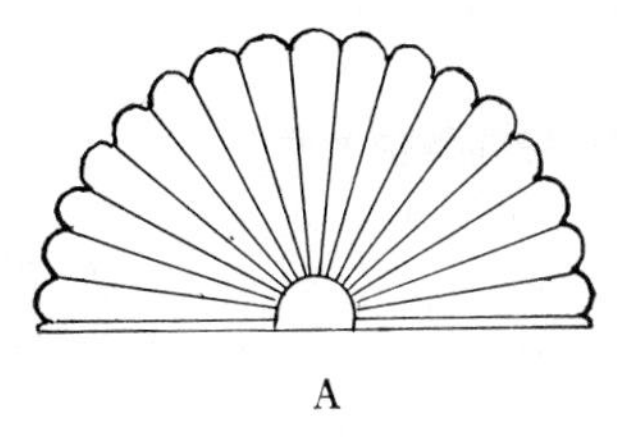

A

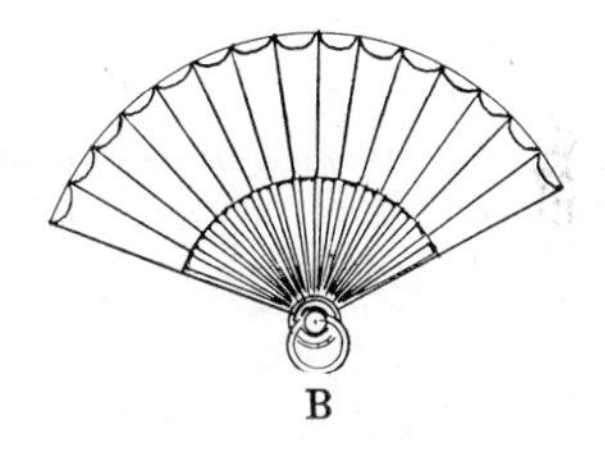

B

Drawing 30.

CARVED ORNAMENTS OF QUEEN ANNE PERIOD

A, sunburst; B, fan. These were used to ornament both highboys and lowboys.

former style. Pieces of this sort were produced by cabinetmakers of all sections.

About 1735 the New England craftsmen struck out and did a little pioneering on their own account. Walnut was replaced by maple, and, in many instances, the drawer fronts and other conspicuous parts were of curly grain (*Illustration 114A*). The top still remained flat, and the arrangement of drawers unchanged. Molding around the drawers, however, was replaced by fronts that had a slight lap finished with a quarter-round beading. Occasionally either a highboy or a lowboy of this type was made with a walnut front and maple sides and legs. The next move was the introduction of a little carving. It was applied to the central drawer of the lower tier in either highboys or lowboys; and this, to accommodate the ornamentation, was made the same depth as the two which flanked it. The design was either a rayed shell or a semicircular fan, and the cutting was incised (*Drawing 30*). There was also some redesigning of the skirt, which was now valanced in outline (*Illustration 114B*). In some of the tall pieces the central drawer of the top tier was also finished with corresponding carving. In either highboys or lowboys of simpler workmanship in these years the carving was replaced by an arched-top depressed panel, and either simple or more elaborate pieces might have their most important surfaces made of curly-grained maple.

The next step affected only the highboy. The flat cornice molding was now replaced by a bonnet top. This was a molded broken-arch pediment executed in cyma curves with finials of conventionalized flame-turning mounted at the front corners and on a pedestal block of curved outline in the centre. (*Illustration 114C.*) With the bonnet-top came a rearrangement of the upper level of drawers. A central one twice the height of those which flanked it was introduced.

Frequently the face of this central drawer was ornamented by a fan carving which balanced that of the similar drawer in the base. In some of the finest pieces of this time—1745 to 1755 are the approximate years—the carving of the central drawers of both top and bottom was more shell-like in execution and was painted and gilded to make this likeness more striking. To say that all of the highboys and lowboys of maple plain or curled of grain were made in New England is too sweeping, but to attribute the best examples to that section is only justice to the craftsmen then working there. Careful study indicates that while cabinetmakers of other localities probably did make these companion pieces in maple or other native woods or even mahogany that were Queen Anne of line and design, the majority were produced in cabinet shops situated within the confines of Connecticut, Massachusetts, New Hampshire, and Rhode Island. Oddly enough, fine examples of these tall and short twins do not seem to have been made by the Townsend-Goddards of Newport. At least none bearing traces of their workmanship have as yet come to light.

In Westchester County, New York, a unique modification

Illustration 115. *(Dr. George P. Coopernail)*

HIGHBOY WITH CLOSET UPPER HALF

Made near Bedford, New York, about 1750 of a combination of woods. The frame is maple; doors, sides, and cornice are of various soft woods. Three highboys of this design have been found in the same general area.

of the flat-topped, Queen Anne highboy was employed (*Illustration 115*). As this territory impinges on Connecticut, it may properly be considered to be of New England as regards this highboy design. The drawer space of the upper section was replaced by a closet equipped with a pair of paneled doors. Whether this was simply the idiosyncrasy of a single craftsman probably working at Bedford or a more general practice within the area, is yet unknown. Having seen three or four examples of this closet highboy, all within the same general section, I am convinced that here is a specialized type; and I do not know of any of its like made elsewhere.

About 1760, supremacy in making both highboys and lowboys forsook New England for Philadelphia. Here for the next fifteen years Savery and contemporaries applied Chippendale lines and ornament with remarkable success (*Illustration 116*). The pieces they made were sophisticated and artistic triumphs. The wood was mahogany, of course, and the cabriole leg with ball-foot replaced the simpler Queen Anne. In structure both pieces were little different from those made earlier. The legs were perhaps a little shorter, and in the highboys, which were now from seven feet six inches to eight feet three tall and up to three feet six inches wide, there was a slight rearrangement of drawers. A typical one had three full-width drawers of graduated depth at the bottom, then one level with three half-width drawers, then one with three drawers, and surmounting the whole a single drawer inserted in the frieze of the bonnet top. This last was of the same width as those just beneath but twice as deep.

The glory of these Philadelphia pieces is in the carving. The ball-and-claw feet (to start at the bottom and progress upward) were boldly done and decorated at the knees with acanthus-leaf carving. The front corners of both highboys and lowboys either were chamfered and fluted or had inset quarter-round fluted pilasters. The skirt was deeply valanced, and generally at the centre there was a shell carved in relief that

(*Metropolitan Museum of Art*)

Illustration 116. (*Metropolitan Museum of Art*)

B

FINE TYPES OF AMERICAN HIGH AND LOWBOYS

Philadelphia pieces made by unknown but master craftsmen in the Chippendale manner. *Ca.* 1760–1770.

might be flanked by shallow leaf-carving. The front of the centre drawer of the lower tier was always decorated with a shell carved in intaglio and circular of outline. The rest of the face of this drawer was given over to leaf-carving which served to frame the shell (*Drawing 31*). The drawer-front ornamentation was repeated in the single one located in the frieze of the bonnet top. The other drawers were unornamented save for the nicely molded quarter-round laps. In the lowboys,

Drawing 31.

CHIPPENDALE SHELL CARVING WITH LEAVES

Such ornamentation is found with practically all highboys and lowboys made by the Philadelphia craftsmen. It was used to decorate the front of the narrow but deep central drawer.

the table top overlapped the structure beneath and was finished on front and sides with molding planed in a rounding curve. In the highboys the curves of the broken arch were boldly scrolled and executed in the same moldings that on the sides served as a flat cornice. At the upper ends of the opposing curves of the bonnet top were placed two carved rosettes done in flower form. At the outer corners there were usually finials of conventionalized flame-pattern; on the central pediment this might be repeated, but more often there was a carved and pierced rococo scroll and cabochon ornament.

These Philadelphia pieces, which in the low and high types

were made for about fifteen years, were quite evidently intended for homes of wealth and taste. They were nothing for a simple farm cottage. Primarily the highboys were so tall that the low-ceilinged rural house could not admit them, and the wealth of carved ornamental detail required a room in which the frames of doors and windows were also treated with carving and elaborate moldings.

Outside of Philadelphia, other craftsmen also made these pieces in the Chippendale manner, but more simply, leaving off the carving. They worked in mahogany and sometimes cherry or apple wood. Both of the latter when varnished have a brownish-red hue that approximates the tone of the former. In short, they made these forms in keeping with their version of other furniture of the Chippendale order just as the highboys and lowboys of Savery were proper pieces to go with ribbon-backed chairs by Randolph and serpentine-fronted chests of drawers by Gostelowe.

The outstanding highboy design of New England was that of Aaron Chapin, who worked until 1783 at East Windsor, Connecticut. His was a combination of Queen Anne lines, Chippendale legs, and a bonnet top that was his own (*Illustration 117*). The curves of the broken pediment sprang from the cornice-molding below and terminated in whorl rosettes. The space between these upward-sweeping curved moldings was filled with a pierced interlacing trelliswork. In the centre there was a short base for the central finial which, like those at the corners, was turned in a baluster form approximating a steeple. Possibly Chapin made highboys a few years longer than the craftsmen of Philadelphia; but certainly they were not of post-Revolutionary production, and probably they were made before Washington took command of the Continental Army beneath the historic elm at Cambridge. The American highboy and its shorter companion—frequently craftsmen made them in pairs—were colonials who did not live to become citizens of the new Republic. After the surrender at Yorktown, Americans, as far as these pieces were

Illustration 117. *(Gallery of Fine Arts, Yale Univ.)*

AN AARON CHAPIN HIGHBOY

The pediment with fret-carved trelliswork and turned baluster finials was his special design. Originally this piece had a central finial like those at the corners but larger. Chapin worked first in East Windsor, Connecticut, and in 1783 moved to Hartford. He made slant-top secretaries with bookcase upper sections to match his highboys.

concerned, had to content themselves with what they might inherit or had already acquired.

From first to last, these pieces were of the fine furniture classification. They were decorative pieces for the well-to-do and never inexpensive. A family struggling for three meals a day could and did get along without them. Therefore the number made was somewhat restricted. Hence the collector who would buy either must expect to pay accordingly. And their use? Lowboys frequently served as tables, either in hall or in dressing room. Just how useful the taller piece was, is not quite clear. Many were employed as display furniture and placed strategically in parlors or main living rooms where they would be seen frequently to the best advantage. Others were probably used in very well-appointed bedrooms. Today, of course, anyone fortunate enough to own either one or the other can place it where he pleases and rest assured that its beauty will be reason enough for its position.

In buying highboys and lowboys collectors can well examine them closely. With the taller piece the things to watch for are replaced legs and an upper section that did not originate with the base. In the 1870's and 1880's the graceful legs of many fine highboys were sawed off to make the piece shorter and less formidable. Where this has been done the only course open to the repairer is to replace them with new legs or possibly splice on new ends. Naturally this lessens the value of the particular piece, however excellent the work. Again tops and bases of highboys will, through the years, get separated, and sometimes a piece is offered in which the upper part has been cut over to correspond to the dimensions of an unrelated base. Both may be old, but the result is an assembly and so is considerably less valuable. With lowboys, in addition to replaced or spliced legs the collector should be sure that a highboy base with top added is not being offered to him. Here again "an eye stored with recollected vision" will pay dividends.

GLOSSARY

APRON. A horizontal strip of wood connecting the upper end of legs or bracket feet. The lower edge of it may be either straight or shaped.

BALUSTER OR BANISTER. A slender turned column swelling outward at points from top to base. Sometimes split vertically and used for the uprights of a chair back.

BANDING. A use of veneer to provide contrast of color or grain between the band and the surface it decorates.

BEAD. A small semi-circular molding either flush with the surrounding surface or raised above it. Sometimes when larger called a cockle bead.

BLOCK FRONT. A treatment of drawer fronts and doors of chests of drawers and secretaries where the two outer panels are flush with the outline of the piece and the center panel depressed.

BONNET TOP. An ornamental curving top of architectural outline used with secretaries, highboys and chests on chests.

BROKEN PEDIMENT. An ornamental top composed of two cyma curves not making a complete sweep.

CABRIOLE. A springing curve applied to legs which swell outward at the knee and inward at the ankle.

CHAMFER. Bevelling of a vertical corner which otherwise would be a right angle.

CROSS RAIL. The horizontal member of a chair back.

CYMA CURVE. A curve of wave-like profile.

DENTIL. A molding made by equally spaced oblong blocks of tooth-like character.

DOWEL. A circular wooden pin used by cabinetmakers to lock a mortice-and-tenon joint.

FINIAL. An ornamental device for finishing corners that projects upward in flame or urn form.

FLUTING. Decorative treatment achieved by grooves or channels. Sometimes referred to as reeding.

FRETTING. Interlaced ornamental detail sometimes applied against a solid background and sometimes perforated.

GALLERY. A raised rim of wooden fretwork or brass surrounding table tops or at the back of sideboard tops.

HOOD. A shaped top found on secretaries, highboys, etc.

INLAY. Wood of contrasting color inset in a decorative pattern.

LADDER BACK. A chair back with horizontal members of greater ornamental shaping than a simple slat.

MORTICE. A rectangular hole cut in wood to receive a tenon.

MOUNTS. The handles, escutcheons and other ornamental metal work decorating a piece of furniture.

OGEE. A form of curve used in moldings in which the convex sides meet in a point.

OVOLO MOLDING. One in which the chief element is oval in contour and frequently convex.
PATINA. The deepened tone of wood resulting from age and wear.
PILASTER. A vertical section of a column used for decorative effect.
RAIL. Horizontal member in cabinetwork or panelling.
REEDING. *See* Fluting.
SERPENTINE FRONT. A front of waving or serpentine curves.
SKIRT. *See* Apron.
SLAT. A simply shaped horizontal member of a chair back.
SPLAT. Central vertical member of a chair back.
STILE. Vertical member in cabinetwork or panelling.
STRETCHER. Cross member used for bracing between chair legs.
SWELL FRONT. A front that curves outward from side to side. Sometimes called bow front.
TAMBOUR. Flexible woodwork made by gluing delicately reeded pieces on a canvas back.
TENON. A tongue of wood cut to fit into a mortice making a mortice-and-tenon joint.
TESTER. A canopy used with tall post beds.
TOP RAIL. The top member of a chair back.
VENEER. Thinly cut wood of ornamental grain glued to plainer wood for decoration.
WAINSCOT. Panel work.

INDEX